10886275

SKILL SHARPENERS
Grammar & Punctuation 1

Manufacturer Evan-Moor Corporation
10 Harris Court, Suite C-3 Monterey, CA 93940, USA
www.evan-moor.com

EU Rep. Authorised Rep Compliance Ltd., Ground Floor,
71 Lower Baggot Street, Dublin, D02 P593, Ireland
www.arccompliance.com

Writing: Rachel D'Orsaneo
Editing: Teera Robinson
Lisa Vitarisi Mathews
Copy Editing: Laurie Westrich
Art Direction: Yuki Meyer
Illustration: Mary Rojas
Design/Production: Paula Acojido
Yuki Meyer
Jessica Onken

EVAN-MOOR
Educational Publishers

EMC 9951

Visit
teaching-standards.com
to view a correlation
of this book.

Correlated to Current Standards

Evan-Moor Corporation
phone 1-800-777-4362, fax 1-800-777-4332.

10 Harris Court, Suite C-3, Monterey, CA 93940-5773. Printed in China.

009

CPSIA: Asia Pacific Offset Ltd, Kowloon, Hong Kong, China [9/2025]

Contents

Weekend Fun! 5

Grammar Concept: Nouns name people, places, animals, and things.

Punctuation Concept: A sentence ends with a period, a question mark, or an exclamation point.

The Five Senses 13

Grammar Concept: Adjectives describe nouns.

Punctuation Concept: Some abbreviations of personal titles end with a period.

School 21

Grammar Concept: Verbs describe the action in a sentence.

Punctuation Concept: An apostrophe replaces a letter or letters so that two words can be joined to form a contraction.

Birthday Party 29

Grammar Concept: Pronouns can replace and function as nouns.

Punctuation Concept: A colon separates the hour and minutes in written time.

Sports 37

Grammar Concept: Proper nouns name specific people, places, animals, and things and are capitalized.

Punctuation Concept: Commas are used after the greetings and closings of friendly letters.

On the Move 45

Grammar Concept: Singular nouns refer to one person, place, animal, or thing, while plural nouns refer to more than one.

Punctuation Concept: Commas are used in dates to separate the day from the year.

Food 53

Grammar Concept: A verb's form must agree with its subject in number.

Punctuation Concept: Commas are used to separate items in a series.

Animals 61

Grammar Concept: A complete sentence has a subject and a predicate.

Punctuation Concept: Titles of books and movies that are written must be underlined.

Family 69

Grammar Concept: Possessive nouns indicate ownership and can be singular or plural.

Punctuation Concept: Apostrophes are used in all possessive nouns, and an apostrophe's placement can indicate whether a possessive noun is singular or plural.

At the Park 77

Grammar Concept: Prepositions can indicate where nouns are located in relation to other nouns.

Punctuation Concept: An abbreviation of a street name ends with a period.

Go and See 85

Grammar Concept: Irregular plural nouns have specific spellings that do not follow a standard rule.

Punctuation Concept: Commas separate the different elements of an address.

The Four Seasons 93

Grammar Concept: Verb tenses indicate the time of an action or state.

Punctuation Concept: Abbreviations of month names end with a period.

With My Friends 101

Grammar Concept: Comparative adjectives compare two nouns, and superlative adjectives compare three or more nouns.

Punctuation Concept: An abbreviation of a day of the week ends with a period.

Bugs and Insects 109

Grammar Concept: Articles precede nouns.

Punctuation Concept: Commas set apart the words *yes* and *no* in sentences.

Pets People Have 117

Grammar Concept: Avoid using double negatives in writing.

Punctuation (Mechanics) Concept: Sentences begin with capital letters.

Language Handbook 125

Remove the Language Handbook on pages 125–130 and staple it together. Use the handbook to remember grammar and punctuation rules.

Answer Key 131

Read the story.

Weekend Fun!

I love the **weekends!** On Saturdays, I help at a pet **shop.** Do you ever take care of **animals?** It is so fun! I give the **dogs** fresh **water.** I play with the **cats.** On Sundays, I help my **mom** around the **house.** Then she makes us **pizza.** Have you ever had pizza? It is so yummy! I am going to bring some to **school** with me on Monday to share with my **friends.**

Read the rules. Answer the questions.

Grammar A **common noun** names a person, place, animal, or thing.

How many green **common nouns** can you find in the story? _____

Punctuation Sentences have **end marks**. A sentence that tells something ends in a (.). A sentence that asks a question ends in a (?). A sentence that tells about something with feeling or excitement ends in a (!).

How many **end marks** can you find in the story?

_____ (.)   _____ (?)   _____ (!)

Concepts:

Nouns name people, places, animals, and things;

A sentence ends with a period, a question mark, or an exclamation point

Weekend Fun!

Skills:
Identify common nouns;
Define common nouns;
Write common nouns

Common Nouns

A **common noun** names a person, place, animal, or thing. A common noun begins with a lowercase letter.

Person	Place	Animal	Thing
girl	school	bird	book
man	home	cat	pie
friend	park	dog	shoe
doctor	shop	fish	bike

Read the sentence. Underline the common noun and write it on the line.

1. This is my house. ______________
2. Do you know that girl? ______________
3. We will go to the park on Saturday! ______________
4. I like to eat pie. ______________
5. Can we ride bikes? ______________

Finish the sentence.

6. A common noun names a

______________________________.

Weekend Fun!

Noun Riddles

Skills:
Write common nouns;
Use clues to solve riddles

The Smiths go to the park on Saturday. They tell riddles in the car on the way there. Read the riddles. Write a common noun to solve each riddle.

1. It is a place where kids go to learn.
   What is it? ________________

2. It is soft, and you wear it on your foot.
   What is it? ________________

3. It is an animal that barks.
   What is it? ________________

4. This is a person who looks at your teeth.
   Who is it? ________________

5. It has two wheels, and you ride it.
   What is it? ________________

Weekend Fun!

Skill:
Produce sentences with end punctuation

End Marks

Every sentence needs an end mark. A sentence that tells about something ends in a period (.).

I like to play with my dog**.**

A sentence that asks a question ends in a question mark (?).

Do you have a dog**?**

Use an exclamation point (!) in a sentence that tells about something with strong feeling or excitement.

My dog can jump and sit**!**

Read. Then write a sentence that tells about something.

1. I ride my bike on Saturdays.

____

____

Read. Then write a sentence that asks a question.

2. Do you play ball on Saturdays?

____

____

Read. Then write a sentence that tells something exciting.

3. I love to sleep in on Sundays!

____

____

Weekend Fun!

Saturday at the Pet Shop

Skill: Identify common nouns

Help the boy get to the pet shop. Color only the boxes with nouns. **REMEMBER:** A noun names a person, place, animal, or thing.

milk	go	sit
cat	sock	park
new	big	frog
book	apple	home
bike	pizza	sad
not	school	dog
feel	happy	pen

Weekend Fun!

Skills:
Identify common nouns;
Write sentences with correct end punctuation

Write It Right!

Fix the sentence. Write it correctly on the lines. Then underline the common noun in the sentence.

1 I went to the dentist on Friday

____

____

2 Can you come to my house on Saturday

____

____

3 We will go to the park

____

____

4 I like to eat pizza on Sundays

____

____

5 Can my friend come over and eat it, too

____

____

Punctuation Match

Draw lines to match the sentences that have the same end marks.

1

Is that a mouse on a bike? •

• I like ice cream!

2

My dog has my sock! •

• There is an owl on my house.

3

I see two cakes. •

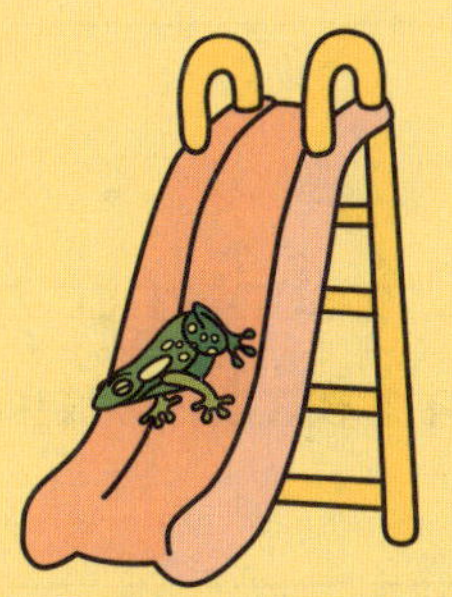

• Is that a frog on the slide?

Skills:

Identify different kinds of end punctuation;

Match

Weekend Fun!

Skills:
Write common nouns;
Use common nouns;
Produce sentences with end punctuation

Sunday at the Beach

Write common nouns from the box to finish the story. Then read the story.

sand	boys	beach	crab

1. My family and I went to the ______________ on Sunday.

2. The ______________ felt hot under my feet!

3. I saw a ______________ on a rock.

4. I saw two ______________ making a sand castle.

Write a sentence that asks a question.
Use a question mark (?) at the end of the sentence.

5. ____

____

____

Write a sentence that tells what you are excited about.
Use an exclamation point (!) at the end of the sentence.

6. ____

____

____

Weekend Fun!

Concepts:
Adjectives describe nouns;
Some abbreviations of personal titles end with a period

Read the story.

A Day at the Farm

I am at Mr. Jim's farm with my class. The farm is **fun**! I see Miss Toro feeding some **little** ducks. I see a **big** horse. I see **spotted** cows eat grass. The ducks like the **cold** water. I hear the animals make **loud** noises. I pet the **tall** horse. Her hair is **soft**. Mr. Jim brushes the horse's hair. I smell something **sweet** coming from the **small** shop near the barn. Mrs. Jane made us a pie. I taste the sweet apples! Yum!

Read the rules. Answer the questions.

Grammar An **adjective** tells more about something or someone. The word **big** is an adjective.

How many **adjectives** can you find in the story? _____

Punctuation Some people have a title before their name. For example: **Mrs.** Lee. The title ends with a **period** (.).

How many orange **periods** after titles can you find? _____

Skill: Identify adjectives

Adjectives

An **adjective** tells about a noun.

Adjectives can tell about size, shape, color, smell, taste, sound, number, and how something feels.

The mouse is **tiny**.

The cake smells **good**.

Look at the picture. Read the words.
Fill in the circle next to the adjective.

1

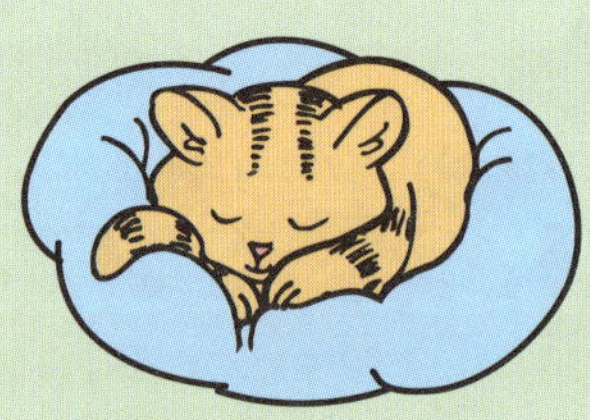

○ kitten ○ little

2

○ three ○ children

3

○ hot ○ sun

4

○ candy ○ sweet

A Day at the Park

Look at the picture. Write an adjective to finish the sentence.

pink **tall** **bumpy** **round**

1. I see the girl go up the ______________ ladder.

2. The bark on the tree feels ______________.

3. The girl will smell the ______________ flower.

4. The boy sits on the ______________ tire swing.

Write a sentence with an adjective.

5. ____

____

Skills:
Write adjectives;
Use adjectives;
Produce a sentence with an adjective

Skills:
Write personal titles with correct punctuation;
Use personal titles;
Use visual information to complete a sentence

Periods in Abbreviations of People's Titles

Some people have a title before their name.
Some titles end with a period (.).

Title
Mr. Yoshi
Mrs. Bozy
Dr. Dunn
Miss Carlito

Write a title to finish the sentence.

Dr. Miss Mr. Mrs.

1. ________ Patel uses his nose to smell the air.

2. ________ Smith washes her hands.

3. ________ Costa bakes cookies.

4. ________ Jones eats a sandwich.

5. ________ Antwon hears a dog barking.

Using Our Senses!

Skills:
Write adjectives;
Use adjectives;
Distinguish between different kinds of adjectives

Write an adjective from the word box to finish the sentence.

See

yellow green

1. The light is ________.

2. I see the ________ frog.

Hear

loud quiet

3. The dog's bark is ________.

4. The mouse's footstep is very ________.

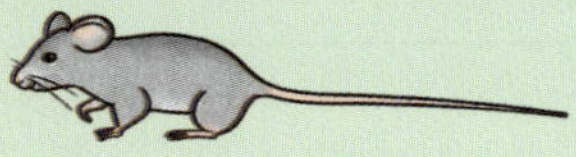

Feel

cold soft

5. The ice cream feels ________.

6. This rabbit feels ________.

Smell

sweet stinky

7. The trash can smells ________.

8. The pie smells ________.

Skills:
Identify incorrect use of adjectives;
Identify punctuation errors in personal titles;
Write sentences using adjectives correctly;
Write sentences using personal titles correctly;
Write personal titles with correct punctuation

Write It Right!

The adjective is in the wrong place in the sentence.
The noun is in the wrong place in the sentence.
Write the sentence to make it correct.

1. The tall is girl.

____

2. The white is milk.

____

3. The good taste nuts.

____

A period is missing in the sentence.
Write the sentence to make it correct.

4. Mr Smith feels cold.

____

5. Dr Cam sees a sick person.

____

6. Mrs Jenner looks friendly.

____

A Picture That Needs a Title!

Look at the picture. Finish the sentences about the picture.
Write a title from the word box.

Mrs. Mr. Dr.

1. ________ Landis feels sick. Her head feels hot.

2. ________ Nam helps ________ Landis to feel better.

3. ________ Tyson waits for ________ Landis. He is her friend.

4. ________ Shore also waits. She feels sick, too.

5. ________ Shore wants ________ Nam to help her feel better, too.

Skills:
Use visual information to complete sentences;
Write personal titles with correct punctuation;
Use personal titles;
Make inferences using visual information

The Five Senses

Skills:
Write adjectives;
Use adjectives;
Produce sentences with personal titles;
Write personal titles using correct punctuation

The Five Senses

Mystery Lunch

Read the story. Write words from the box to finish the story.

salty	yellow	hot	soft

1. Jim's lunch looks ________. Jim takes a bite. The food burns his lips because it is ________. Jim waits for it to get cool. Then he takes another bite. The food tastes ________. The noodles feel ________ when he chews them. What is Jim eating? It's macaroni and cheese!

Write a sentence. Use the word **Mr.** in your sentence.

2. ____

____

Write a sentence. Use the word **Mrs.** in your sentence.

3. ____

____

Read the story.

School Days

School is awesome! I **see** my friends every day because they're in my class. We've got a pet crab in my classroom. We can't feed him too much! If we do, he'll get sick. We **love** him.

Everyone at school is nice. Mr. James is my teacher. He's really smart. He **teaches** us new things. I like it when we **learn** math. After we do work, we'll go to recess. My friend Anna and I **play** together. She's my best friend. School is so fun. I **kick** the soccer ball. I love school days.

Concepts:
Verbs describe the action in a sentence;
An apostrophe replaces a letter or letters so that two words can be joined to form a contraction

Read the rules. Answer the questions.

Grammar A **verb** tells what someone or something does.

How many purple **verbs** can you find in the story? _____

Punctuation A contraction is two words made into one word. We use a ' in contractions. The ' connects two words.

How many 's can you find in the story? _____

Skill:
Identify verbs

Verbs

A **verb** is an action word.

A verb tells what someone or something does.

The teacher **adds** numbers.

The student **asks** a question.

The kids **play** kickball.

Read the sentence. Underline the action word.

1. The children sing songs.
2. James reads a book.
3. The teacher writes a note.
4. Dylan sits at his desk.
5. Sarah uses the blocks.
6. Debbie draws a picture.
7. The children talk in line.
8. Chelsea plays a math game.

After School

Skills:
Write verbs;
Use verbs

Look at the picture. Finish the sentence with a verb from the pencil.

rides play throws write sits eat

1

Jane __________ in a chair.

2

Eduardo __________ his bike to school.

3

The boys __________ their food.

4

Dan __________ the ball to Aaron.

Skills:
Match;
Identify contractions;
Recognize words that form specific contractions

Apostrophes in Contractions

A contraction is two words made into one word.
An **apostrophe** (’) takes the place of the missing letters.

was not ⟶ was n~~o~~t ⟶ wasn’t

can not ⟶ can ~~no~~t ⟶ can’t

Draw a line to match the words to the contraction. Trace the apostrophe.

1. did not •	• he’s
2. are not •	• I’m
3. he is •	• didn’t
4. I am •	• aren’t

Read the sentence. Circle the contraction.

5. She’s having fun on a swing.

School

Skill: Identify verbs

The Verbs on the Bus

Help the buses get to school. Color only the windows that have verbs. A bus must have all its windows colored to get to school.

Which buses made it to school?
Circle the letters.

A B C

Skills:

Identify incorrect use of verbs;

Write sentences using verbs correctly;

Identify apostrophe errors in contractions;

Write apostrophes to correct contractions

Write It Right!

The verb is in the wrong place in the sentence.
Write the sentence to make it correct.

EXAMPLE: Wrong: Pat on the floor **sits.**
Right: Pat **sits** on the floor.

1. Jimmy the book reads.

____

2. Tracy her hand up puts.

____

3. Abe and Sherry books carry.

____

An apostrophe is missing in each sentence.
Write the apostrophe in the sentence.

4. Dom cant find his pencil.

5. Ill hang up her coat.

6. Theyre walking to school.

Contractions Need Apostrophes!

Skills:
Recognize words that form specific contractions;
Identify contractions

Draw lines to connect two words to the matching contraction. Then write an apostrophe in the contraction. The first one is done for you.

should	did	not
not	shouldn't	didnt
you	youll	dont
will	do	not

School

Skills:
Produce sentences with verbs;
Identify verbs;
Form contractions with correct punctuation

All About Verbs and Apostrophes in Contractions

Write two sentences about what you do at school.
Circle the verb in each sentence.

1. ____

____

2. ____

____

Put the words together to make a contraction.
Write the contraction on the line. Remember to use an apostrophe (’).

3. can not ______________

4. would not ______________

5. should not ______________

6. is not ______________

7. she will ______________

8. have not ______________

School

Read the story.

A Birthday Party

Today is Ryan's birthday party. Ryan invited all his friends to the party. **He** told **me** that the party starts at 3**:**00. **It** is 1**:**00 now. There will be pizza, cake, and balloons at the party. **I** will see Danielle. **She** is also Ryan's friend. I will bring Ryan a birthday gift. I hope he will like it. At 2**:**00, Mom and I wrap the gift together. **We** will put a ribbon on it. I can't wait for the party!

Read the rules. Answer the questions.

Grammar A **pronoun** is a word that can take the place of a noun in a sentence.

How many blue **pronouns** can you find in the story? _____

Punctuation When we write the time, we use a **colon** **:** between the hour and the minutes.

How many **colons** can you find in the story? _____

Concepts:

Pronouns can replace and function as nouns;

A colon separates the hour and minutes in written time

Birthday Party

Skill:
Match correct pronouns to correct antecedents

Pronouns

A **pronoun** is a word that takes the place of a noun.

I you he she it him her

A girl opens a present. **She** opens a present.

Some **pronouns** take the place of more than one noun.

we they us them

The boys and girls sang! **They** sang!

Read the sentence. Look at the underlined word or words. Circle the correct pronoun to take the place of the noun or nouns.

1. Eddie eats cake.	She	He	It
2. Toby and I get balloons.	They	Us	We
3. The cake is green.	We	It	You
4. Trang gave Sara a birthday hat.	we	her	them
5. Bashar and Amy open gifts.	Us	He	They
6. I saw Joe and Sue at the party.	you	him	them

The Perfect Pronoun

Look at the underlined word or words in the sentence.
Write a pronoun to take the place of the common or proper noun.

I You He She It We They

1. Zoey and Jaya dance along with the music.

   _______________ dance along with the music.

2. Pablo and I play a game at the party.

   _______________ play a game at the party.

3. The girl invited her friends.

   _______________ invited her friends.

Write a sentence with the pronoun **he**.

4. ____

   ____

Skills:
Write pronouns;
Match correct pronouns to correct antecedents;
Produce a sentence using a pronoun

Birthday Party

Skill:
Write colons in time

Colons in Time

When you write the time, use a **colon** (:) between the numbers that show the hour and the minutes.

The birthday party begins at 3:00.

We will cut the cake at 4:00.

The party ends at 5:00.

Read the sentence.
Write the colon in the time.

1. Jake leaves for the party at 2___00.
2. Mia leaves for the party at 2___30.
3. Timmy gets to John's house at 3___00.
4. John blows out the candles at 4___40.
5. John opens gifts at 5___15.
6. The children play games at 5___30.
7. All of John's friends leave at 6___20.
8. John goes to bed at 8___10.

Pronoun Match

Skill:
Use visual information to identify correct pronouns

Read the sentences. Fill in the circle next to the sentence that matches the picture.

1

- ○ She grabs balloons.
- ○ They grab balloons.

2

- ○ He blows out the candles.
- ○ We blow out the candles.

3

- ○ She makes a birthday wish.
- ○ He makes a birthday wish.

4

- ○ The clown juggles us in the air.
- ○ The clown juggles them in the air.

Skills:
Identify incorrect pronouns;
Identify punctuation errors in time;
Write correct pronouns;
Write colons in time correctly

Write It Right!

Read the sentences. The second sentence has the wrong pronoun. Write the correct pronoun on the line.

1. Jim, Alexis, and Hector are here.
   It have gifts. ____________

2. Dad gets pizza for the party.
   She asks for cheese pizzas. ____________

3. The party was fun!
   They was at the park. ____________

The time is not written correctly in the sentence. Write the time correctly on the line.

4. Hudson opened his birthday gifts at 5 15. __________

5. Shivani ate cake and ice cream at 7 30. __________

6. Donatello took a shower at 12 00. __________

Fix the Watch

Skill: Write colons in time

Terrell got a new watch as a birthday gift, but something is wrong with it. Write (:)s to fix the way it shows the time.

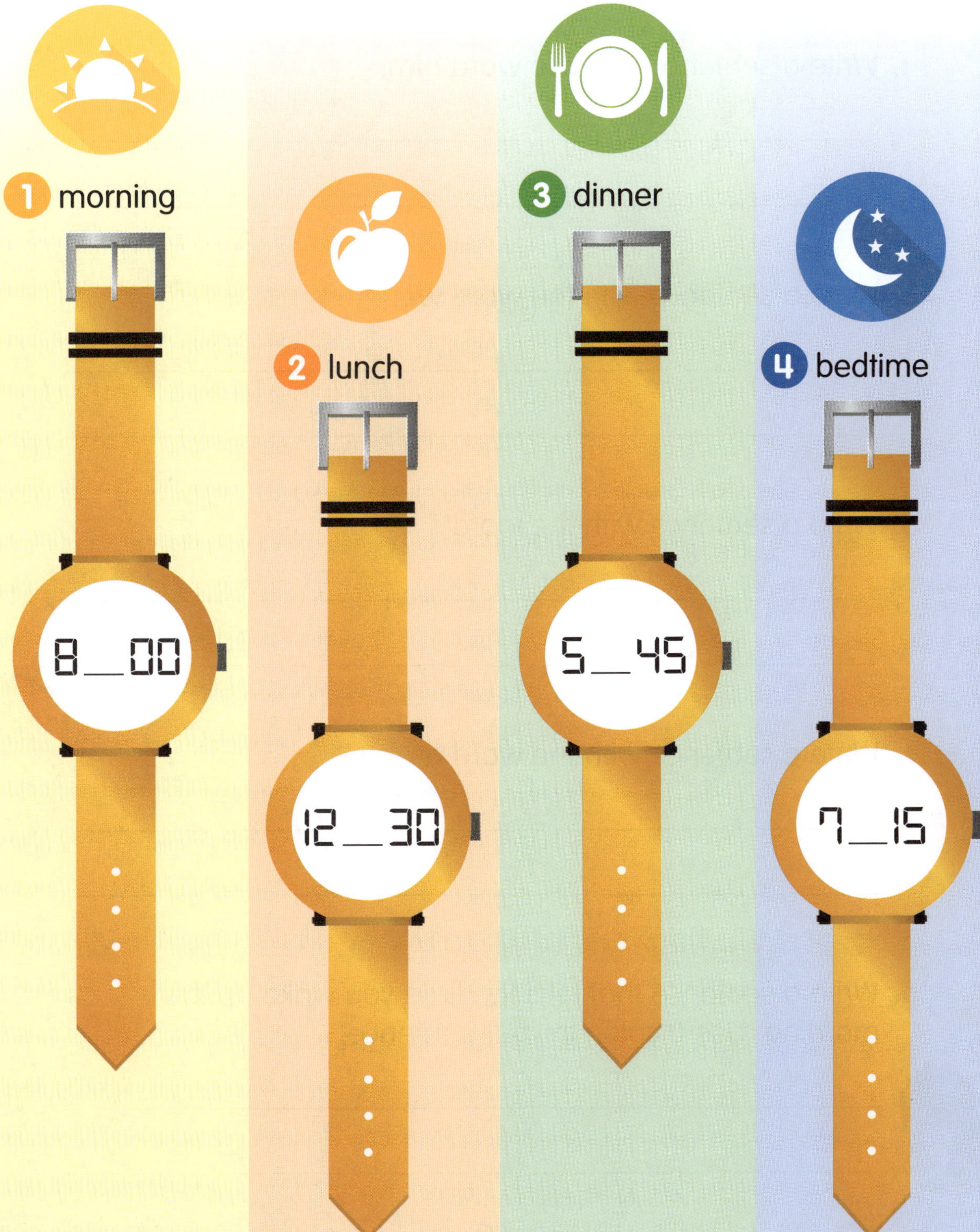

Skills:
Produce sentences using pronouns;
Produce a sentence using a colon in time

All About Pronouns and Colons

Write sentences about a birthday party.

1. Write a sentence with the word **him**.

____

____

2. Write a sentence with the word **we**.

____

____

3. Write a sentence with the word **I**.

____

____

4. Write a sentence with the word **us**.

____

____

5. Write a sentence that tells the time you woke up this morning. Use a colon in your sentence.

____

____

Read the letter.

A Letter to the Best Soccer Player Ever!

Dear Keegan Jorgan,

Soccer is a cool sport. I play soccer on a team. I started playing last year. My coach is Mrs. Foster. My brother, Charles, also plays soccer. His team is called The Allstars. I want to play soccer when I grow up, like you do. Do you have any tips for me? On Friday, I have a game in a town called Berryview. Wish me luck!

From,

Emily Sherman

Read the rules. Answer the questions.

Grammar A **proper noun** names someone or something. A proper noun starts with a capital letter. The names of people, places, animals, and things are proper nouns. Hint: Keegan Jorgan = 1 proper noun

How many **proper nouns** can you find? _____

Punctuation We use **commas** , after the greetings and closings of friendly letters.

How many orange **commas** can you find? _____

Concepts:

Proper nouns name specific people, places, animals, and things and are capitalized;

Commas are used after the greetings and closings of friendly letters

Sports

Skills:
Identify proper nouns;
Write proper nouns correctly

Proper Nouns

A **proper noun** names a person, place, animal, or thing. A proper noun begins with a capital letter.

Person	**Gina Smith** likes to swim.
Place	She lives in **Florida**.
Animal	Her pet fish is named **Swimmy**.

Read the sentence.
Circle the proper noun.

1. My name is Mario.
2. I live on Tennis Street.
3. My uncle lives in the town of Hilly.
4. Uncle Jeff plays ball.

Read the sentence. Write the underlined word correctly on the line.

5. My brother's name is <u>alex</u>. ______________
6. He plays sports in <u>india</u>. ______________

Table Tennis

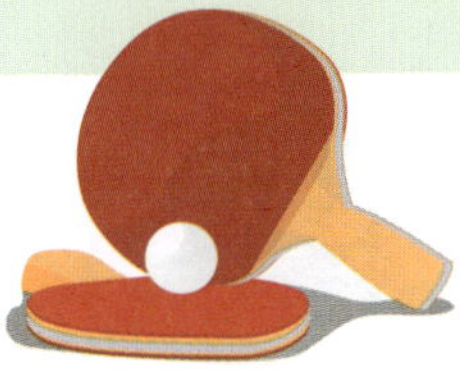

Skills:
Identify proper nouns;
Write a proper noun correctly

A **proper noun** names someone or something. A proper noun begins with a capital letter.

Day	My game is on **Tuesday**.
Month	I will play ball in **February**.
Holiday	Japan has a holiday called **Sports Day**.

Read the sentence. Circle the proper noun.

1. Ethan Wong plays table tennis with his family.

2. They play on holidays like Chinese New Year.

3. They play every Sunday.

4. They have a neighborhood game every May.

Read the sentence. Write the underlined word correctly on the line.

5. Can we skip table tennis on <u>friday</u>? ____________

Skill:
Write commas in greetings and closings of friendly letters

Commas in Greetings and Closings of Letters

Use a **comma** (,) in the greeting of a letter.
Use a comma in the closing of a letter.

Greeting: Dear Jane,

Closing: From,
Dan

Write a comma in the greeting of the letter and in the closing of the letter.

1.

July 7, 2020

Dear Mrs. Smith

Thank you for helping me at swim camp. I had a great time!

Yours truly

Leo Martinez

2.

January 8, 2020

Dear Uncle Tommy

My birthday party is very soon. Will you be able to come over?

Your niece

Tia

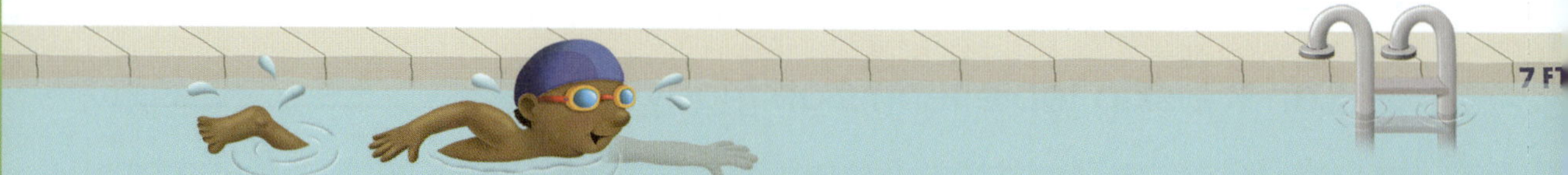

Lots of Letters

Read the friendly letter. Circle the friendly letter if it has commas where they belong.

1. (b)

Jane,
How are you?
From,
Tom

2. (z)

Kelly
What did you do today?
Love
Mom

3. (p)

Chris
I miss you!
Your sister
Pam

4. (k)

Tony
What is your address?
With love
Aunt Bertha

5. (t)

Jeremy,
The game is at 4:00 on Monday.
Sincerely,
Bill

6. (a)

Tori,
What is your favorite sport?
From,
Lola

RIDDLE: What kind of animal do you need to play baseball?

To solve the riddle, use the purple letters above the friendly letters you circled. Write the letters so they form a word on the lines.

You need a _____ _____ _____!

Skills:

Use clues to solve a riddle;

Identify correct and incorrect punctuation in the greetings and closings of friendly letters;

Write commas to correct the punctuation in the greetings and closings of friendly letters

Sports

Skills:

Produce friendly letters using correct punctuation;

Write commas in the greetings and closings of friendly letters;

Use proper nouns using correct capitalization

Write a Letter

Write a letter to your teacher about a holiday you like. Use correct capitalization. Remember to put commas where they belong.

1.

July 6, 2020

Dear

From

Write a letter to your friend about your birthday. Tell when your birthday is. Remember to put commas where they belong.

2.

September 23, 2020

Dear

From

Read the story.

Concepts:
Singular nouns refer to one person, place, animal, or thing, while plural nouns refer to more than one;
Commas are used in dates to separate the day from the year

Planes, Planes, Planes

Have you ever been on a **plane**? I have! My first time was on Wednesday, January 10**,** 2018. It was so much fun! I could see the **clouds**. The **people** on the ground looked like little **dots**. I will fly to Disney World on March 4**,** 2019. We will drive our **car** to the **airport**. Then, off we will go! I will get lots of **snacks** to eat on the plane.

Read the rules. Answer the questions.

Grammar Some **nouns** name one person or thing. Some **nouns** name more than one.

How many blue **nouns** in the story name one? _____

How many green **nouns** name more than one? _____

Punctuation We use **commas in dates** **,** between the day and the year.

How many orange **commas in dates** can you find? _____

Skills:

Identify singular and plural nouns;

Use visual information to distinguish between singular and plural nouns

On the Move

Singular and Plural Nouns

A **noun** can name one or more than one.
Add **s** to some nouns to name more than one.

Louis has one **truck**. Lila has two **trucks**.

Nate has one **boat**. Lovey has two **boats**.

Does the noun name one or more than one?
Circle the correct picture.

1. trucks  

2. train  

3. cars  

4. boat  

Singular or Plural?

A **noun** can name one or more than one.
Singular nouns name one person or thing.
Plural nouns name more than one.
Add **es** to some nouns to name more than one.

Benito uses a **brush.**

The children use **brushes.**

Nadia rides the bus with her dad. She sees many things as she looks out the window. Circle the noun that goes with the picture.

1. 

box boxes

2. 

bench benches

3. 

bus buses

4. 

bush bushes

Skills:
Write commas in dates;
Produce a sentence with a date;
Write a date using correct punctuation

Commas in Dates

Use a **comma** , between the day and year in a date.
The boat will sail on March 13**,** 2020.

Read the sentence. Write a comma between the day and the year.

1. We will ride the train on July 9 2020.
2. Our family trip starts on July 8 2020.
3. Dad got the train tickets on June 23 2020.
4. We will go on a plane on July 20 2020.
5. We will return home on a bus on August 4 2020.

Write a sentence that tells a date with the month, day, and year. Use a comma.

6. ____

____

Help the Plane

Help the plane fly to one of the airports. The plane will only fly over clouds with plural nouns. Color the clouds that the plane will fly over.

Which airport did the plane land at? ______________________________

Skills:

Use visual information to distinguish between singular and plural nouns;

Identify singular and plural nouns

Draw;

Show understanding of singular and plural nouns

Skills:
Identify punctuation errors in dates;
Write commas correctly in dates;
Identify singular and plural nouns

Write It Right!

Read the sentence. Write a comma if it is needed. Then write **one** or **more than one** to tell about the underlined noun.

1. I got a new wagon on April 7 2017. ________
2. I see two rafts on the lake. ________
3. We'll get bikes on June 8 2020. ________
4. The boat was on the river on July 2 2017. ________
5. Can we get a new car? ________

What Carl Did

Read the story.

Carl rode on a bus on Friday. Friday was March 2, 2019. He rode a bike the next day, on Saturday. He rode on a boat on Sunday.

Skills:

Use a calendar to determine a date;

Write dates using correct punctuation;

Draw

Write the date to finish the sentence.
Then draw a picture of what Carl did that day.

1. The date on Saturday was ______________________.

2. The date on Sunday was ______________________.

Skills:
Use visual information to distinguish between singular and plural nouns;
Write singular and plural nouns;
Use singular and plural nouns;
Write dates using correct punctuation;
Use a calendar

On the Road, in the Sky

Look at the picture. Write the correct noun to finish the sentence.

1.

There are 3 ____________ on the road.
car cars

2.

There is a ____________ on the tracks.
train trains

3.

The ____________ is up in the sky.
plane planes

Read Robert's calendar. Write the date to answer the question. Remember to use a comma where it is needed.

Robert			October 2019			
Sunday	**Monday**	**Tuesday**	**Wednesday**	**Thursday**	**Friday**	**Saturday**
1	2 Pick apples	3	4 John's birthday	5 Go fishing	6	7 Ride the ferry

4. On what date did Robert go fishing? ____________________

5. What date did Robert ride the ferry? ____________________

Concepts:
A verb must agree with its subject in number;
Commas are used to separate items in a series

Read the story.

Family and Food

I have a big family. We **love** food. Dave **loves** to eat fruit. He **eats** apples, bananas, and oranges every day. Mom and Dad **eat** lots of carrots, beans, and peas. Grandma **likes** sweets. My cousins **like** eggs. We **shop** at the store. That's where my big sisters **get** gum, juice, and bread. Grandpa **gets** berries, milk, and crackers. There are so many good foods to eat!

Read the rules. Answer the questions.

Grammar A **singular verb** tells what one person does. A **plural verb** tells what more than one person does.

How many purple **singular verbs** can you find in the story? ______

How many green **plural verbs** can you find in the story? ______

Punctuation Write a **comma** , between each word in a list.

How many **commas** with words in a list can you find in the story? ______

Food

Skills:

Write singular and plural verbs;

Ensure subject-verb agreement;

Use singular and plural verbs

Verbs

A **verb** tells what one person or thing does. A verb can also tell what more than one person or thing does.

One:	Jay **eats.**	The dog **eats.**
More than one:	Jay and Tom **eat.**	The dogs **eat.**

Look at the picture. Write the correct verb on the line to finish the sentence.

1. Mom ____________ food for dinner.
   chops chop

2. Kyle and Dad ____________ with their food.
   plays play

3. Mom and Dad ____________ a story at dinner.
   hears hear

4. The baby ____________ eating.
   loves love

Food

What Do You Eat at School?

Read the sentence. Write the correct verb on the line.

Skills:
Write singular and plural verbs;
Ensure subject-verb agreement;
Use singular and plural verbs;
Produce a sentence using subject-verb agreement;
Produce a sentence using a plural subject and verb

1. Tanya ______________ lunch in a brown bag.
   brings   bring

2. Ray and Denzel ______________ by the door at lunch.
   sits   sit

3. Mom ______________ a yummy lunch for Kenny.
   makes   make

4. Prisha and Jamie ______________ on crackers.
   munches   munch

5. Mrs. Wong ______________ Mario open his milk.
   helps   help

Write a sentence with a verb that tells about more than one.

6. ____

____

Food

Skills:

Use commas to separate items in a series;

Produce a sentence with a series using correct punctuation;

Use visual information to produce a sentence

Commas with Words in a List

Use a **comma** , between words in a list.
Write a comma before the word **and**.

My sister bakes cookies**,** cakes**,** and pies.

She uses milk**,** butter**,** salt**,** and sugar.

Read the sentence. It is missing commas.
Write a comma between each word in a list.

1. I pack lunch on Monday Tuesday and Friday.

2. Every day I eat toast fruit cheese and yogurt.

3. Janet washes her spoon fork and plate.

Look at the picture. Write a sentence that tells three things you see. Write a comma between each thing.

4. ____

____

Food

Food, Food, Food

Read the sentence. Write the correct verb.
Then draw a line to match the picture to the sentence.

1. 

2. 

3. 

4. 

- They ____________ dinner.
  eat eats

- They ____________ together.
  shop shops

- Dante ____________ the cake batter.
  stir stirs

- She ____________ at the food on the plate.
  look looks

Skills:
Use visual information to match;
Write singular and plural verbs;
Ensure subject-verb agreement;
Use singular and plural verbs

Food

Skills:

Identify errors in subject-verb agreement;

Identify missing commas in a series;

Write singular and plural verbs to correct subject-verb agreement errors;

Use commas to correctly separate items in a series

Write It Right!

The sentence has the wrong verb.
Write the correct verb on the line.

1. Jan shop for food. ____________

2. The hot dogs looks yummy. ____________

3. Kim and Yun makes dinner. ____________

Write the missing commas in the sentence.

4. I eat an egg toast and a banana in the morning.

5. My family has juice pasta salad and bread at dinner.

Three Foods

Look at the pictures. Follow the directions.

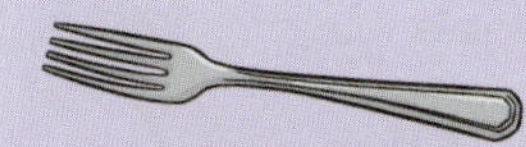
fork

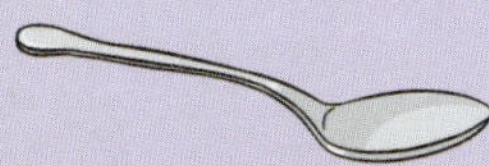
spoon

bowl

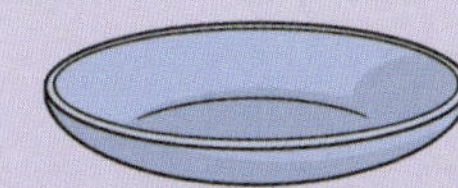
plate

1. Write a sentence that lists three things in the pictures that you have at your house. Use commas.

____

____

sandwich

milk

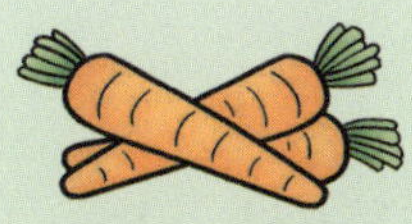
carrot sticks

crackers

2. Write a sentence that lists three foods in the pictures that you would eat for lunch. Use commas.

____

____

cake

ice cream cone

berries

pie

3. Write a sentence that lists three foods in the pictures that you would eat for dessert. Use commas.

____

____

Skills:

Produce sentences with series using correct punctuation;

Use visual information to produce sentences;

Use commas to separate items in a series

Skills:

Identify correct and incorrect use of subject-verb agreement;

Identify correct and incorrect use of commas to separate items in a series

All About Food

Read the sentence. Is the verb correct? Circle **yes** or **no.**

1. Dale needs bread and milk.

   yes no

2. Mickey eat a lot.

   yes no

3. Lindsey writes a book about food.

   yes no

Read the sentence. Are there commas in the right place? Circle **yes** or **no.**

4. Burt wants peas carrots and rice.

   yes no

5. Blake finds a spoon, bowl, fork, and plate.

   yes no

Read the text.

Animal Movies

What makes a movie good? Animals! **People like animal movies**. There is a movie called Air Bud. **The movie tells about a dog**. **The dog plays basketball**. Can you believe that? There is another movie named The Lion King. The lion makes friends with other animals. There are lots of good animal movies. Another one is called A Bug's Life. It is about bugs. **The bugs talk in that movie**. I love it when animals talk!

Read the rules. Answer the questions.

Grammar A sentence has a **naming part** and a **telling part**. The telling part is the verb and everything that comes after it.

How many blue **naming parts** can you find in the text? _____

How many green **telling parts** can you find in the text? _____

Punctuation **Underline titles**, or names, of books and movies.

How many **underlined titles** can you find in the text? _____ **titles**

Concepts:

A complete sentence has a subject and a predicate;

Titles of books and movies that are written must be underlined

Skills:
Match a subject to its predicate;
Produce a complete sentence

Sentence Parts (Subject and Predicate)

A **sentence** tells a complete thought or idea.

This is a sentence	This is not a sentence
Some dogs bark a lot.	Some dogs.
Hamsters make cute sounds.	Make cute sounds.

Draw a line. Connect the two parts that make a sentence.

1. Birds • • bark at things.
2. Dogs • • like to play and swing.
3. Monkeys • • say meow a lot.
4. Cows • • fly over us.
5. Cats • • eat grass.

Write a sentence about your favorite animal.

6. ______________________________

____

Is a Part Missing?

Skills:
Identify incomplete and complete sentences;
Identify subjects and predicates

Every sentence has a naming part. The **naming part** tells who or what the sentence is about.

A hippo rests in mud.

Every sentence has a telling part. The **telling part** tells what happens in the sentence.

The tiger **swims in the river.**

Read the words. Is there a naming part? Circle **yes** or **no**.

1. To the river. yes no
2. A mother hippo looks at a baby hippo. yes no
3. Eats fish. yes no

Read the words. Is there a telling part? Circle **yes** or **no**.
If there is a telling part, draw a line under it.

4. The tiger. yes no
5. A tiger hunts in the grass. yes no
6. Tigers jump up high. yes no

Skills:

Identify book and movie titles;

Underline book and movie titles;

Produce a sentence with a book or movie title using correct punctuation

Underline Titles of Books and Movies

Underline the title of a book or movie.

You can read the book called **About Dogs**.

You can watch the movie called **Finding Nemo**.

Underline the book title or movie title in the sentence.

1. The book called My Wild Animal World tells facts about animals.
2. You can watch a movie called Animals Are Beautiful People.
3. Many children like the book Peek Inside the Zoo.
4. The Shaggy Dog is an old movie.

Answer the question. Underline the title of the book or movie in your answer.

5. What book do you like?

____

____

6. What movie do you like?

____

____

Animal Maze

Draw a line through the complete sentences to get to the end of the maze.

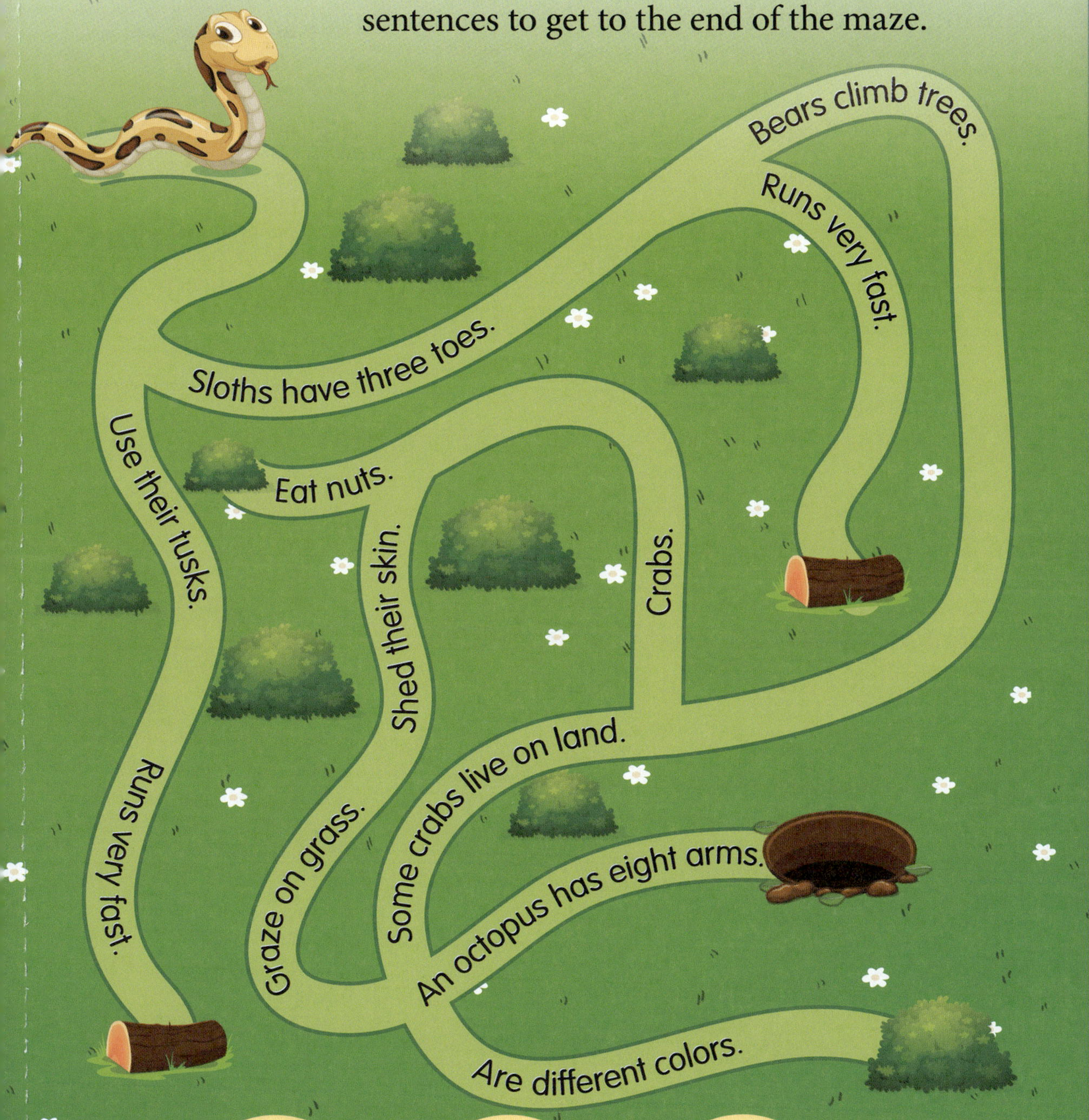

Circle the animals that can't fit in the hole in the maze.

bear crab snake cow

Skills:

- Identify incomplete and complete sentences;
- Identify subjects and predicates;
- Use visual information to answer a question;
- Practice spatial awareness

Animals

Skills:

Identify subjects and predicates;

Write the title of a book or movie using correct punctuation;

Identify book and movie titles

Write It Right!

The sentences have a part missing. Circle **naming part** or **telling part** to show what is <u>missing</u>.

1. The whale. naming part telling part
2. Sits in the mud. naming part telling part
3. All the cows. naming part telling part

The sentence has a title that is written incorrectly. Write the title correctly on the line.

4. You can see the movie called The Secret Life of Pets.

____

5. The book Dogs and Puppies has a lot of facts.

____

6. The movie Stuart Little is about a mouse.

____

What's the Title?

This picture is from a book. Write a good title for the book. Remember to underline the title. Then write a sentence about the picture.

Title:

____

____

Sentence:

____

____

Draw a picture of your favorite animal movie. Write the title. Remember to underline the title. Then write a sentence about the movie.

Title:

____

____

Sentence:

____

____

Skills:

Write a book or movie title using correct punctuation;

Use visual information to write a title;

Produce a sentence in context;

Draw

Animals

Skills:

Use visual information to write a predicate and complete a sentence;

Use visual information to write subjects and complete sentences;

Identify subjects and predicates;

Produce a complete sentence with a book title using correct punctuation

At the Farm

Look at the picture. Then use a word group from the box to finish each sentence about the picture.

Word Box

The zebras

sprays the zebras with water

The water

1. The elephant ______________________________.

2. ______________________ get wet in the water.

3. ______________________ makes a puddle on the ground.

Write one sentence about a book you like.
Remember to underline the title.

4. ____

____

Read the story.

Our Big Sale!

My **family's** yard sale is tomorrow! We have one every year. We sell a lot of stuff that we do not use anymore. Let me tell you what is for sale. My **dad's** fishing pole is five dollars. My **mom's** fish tank is six dollars. My **sisters'** bikes are ten dollars. My **brother's** toy car is two dollars. My two **dogs'** leashes are one dollar each. My **parents'** hats are four dollars each. I hope a lot of people come over to buy our stuff!

Read the rules. Answer the questions.

Grammar A **singular possessive noun** shows that something belongs to one person, animal, or thing. A **plural possessive noun** shows that something belongs to more than one person, animal, or thing.

How many **singular possessive nouns** can you find? _____

How many **plural possessive nouns** can you find? _____

Punctuation Possessive nouns always have an **apostrophe** (').

How many **apostrophes** can you find? _____

Find It!

Concepts:
Possessive nouns indicate ownership and can be singular or plural;
Apostrophes are used in all possessive nouns, and an apostrophe's placement can indicate whether a possessive noun is singular or plural

Family

Skills:
Identify possessive nouns;
Show understanding of a possessive noun

Possessive Nouns

A **possessive noun** shows that something belongs to a person, animal, or thing.
It has an **apostrophe** ’.

My **dad’s** hat is red.

The hat belongs to my dad.

Circle the possessive noun in the sentence.

1. Mom’s hair is brown.
2. Rick’s arm is broken.
3. My sister is at Dana’s house.
4. Granny’s house smells like cookies.
5. My dog’s tail is short.
6. Where is John’s book?

Read the sentence. Then answer the question.

7. Mom’s hair is long!

   To whom does the hair belong?

   ____

Family

Plural Possessive Nouns

Skill:
Use visual information to show understanding of possessive nouns

A **plural possessive noun** shows that something belongs to **more than one** person, animal, or thing. Many plural possessive nouns end with a ’.

The **twins’** shirts are blue.

The shirts belong to the twins.

Read the words. Fill in the circle to tell about the picture.

1. the girls’ shoes

○

○

2. The dogs’ bowls

○

○

3. the cats’ yarn

○

○

4. the boys’ ball

○

○

Family

Skills:

Write apostrophes in possessive nouns;

Form possessive nouns

Apostrophes with Possessives

We put an **apostrophe** (’) and an **s** at the end of most nouns to make them possessive. When a plural noun ends in **s**, we put only an **apostrophe** at the end to make it possessive.

Singular: The boy**’s** coat is small.

Plural: The boys**’** coats are small.

Write (’) or (’) and **s** to show that something belongs to someone.

1. Where is Zayne_____ cup?
2. The beds_____ pillows are all clean.
3. The cats_____ toys are in the basket.
4. Have you seen Grandma_____ pen?
5. Aunt Elise made the girls_____ snack.

Match It!

Draw a line to match the words to the correct picture.

1. my brother's glasses •

2. my sisters' book •

3. my brothers' glasses •

4. my sister's book •

Look at the picture. Then circle the words that go with the picture.

5

childrens backpacks

children's backpacks

Skills:
Use visual information to show understanding of possessive nouns;
Match

Family

Skills:
Identify possessive nouns;
Identify punctuation errors in possessive nouns;
Form possessive nouns with correct punctuation;
Use apostrophes in possessive nouns

Family

Application

Write It Right!

Read the sentence. Is the possessive noun correct? Circle **yes** or **no**.

1. My moms shoes are orange. yes no
2. Where are Vince's glasses? yes no
3. Our familys van is messy. yes no

The possessive noun in the sentence is not correct. Write it correctly on the line.

4. Papas pen is on the table. ______________
5. We put up my four uncles pictures. ______________

Look at the Apostrophes

Look at the picture. Fill in the circle next to the words that tell about the picture.

1

- ○ Auntie Claire's hat
- ○ Auntie Claires hat

2

- ○ the kitten's baskets
- ○ the kittens' baskets

3

- ○ the cake's candles
- ○ the cakes' candles

4

- ○ the flower's petals
- ○ the flowers' petals

Skills:

Use visual information to show understanding of possessive nouns;

Use apostrophe placement to distinguish between different meanings of possessive nouns

Skills:

Write apostrophes correctly in possessive nouns;

Form possessive nouns;

Use apostrophes in possessive nouns

Whose Is It?

Read the sentence. Write an apostrophe in the possessive noun.

1. Dads mug has white dots.
2. Moms mug looks like a rainbow.
3. Auntie Erins mug has flowers.
4. My grandparents mugs are yellow.
5. My two sisters mugs are mostly pink.

Look at the family's mugs. The sentences above have clues to tell you who each mug belongs to. Write a possessive noun to tell whose mug it is.

6. ________________ mug

7. ________________ mug

8. ________________ mug

9. ________________ mugs

Concepts:
Prepositions can indicate where nouns are located in relation to other nouns;
An abbreviation of a street name ends with a period

Read the story.

A Walk in the Park

My family and I went **to** a big park **in** the city. I had a lot **of** fun. The park is **on** Toby St. **near** a school. My brother and I ran **across** a big green lawn. We ran to the slide. Then we stood near hoops where kids were playing ball. **After** the park, we went to a shop on Kin Dr. to get hot dogs. It was **by** a bus stop. Then we went back to our house **at** 414 Day Rd. in Lake Town.

Abbreviations

Street = St.

Drive = Dr.

Road = Rd.

Read the rules. Answer the questions.

Grammar A **preposition** is a word that connects a noun or a pronoun to other words in a sentence.

How many purple **prepositions** can you find in the story? ______

Punctuation We can make a street name shorter by using an abbreviation. We use a **period** (.) after a street name abbreviation.

How many orange **periods** with abbreviations of street names can you find above? ______

Skills:
Write prepositions;
Use prepositions;
Distinguish between prepositions with different meanings

Prepositions

Some words that tell **where** are called **prepositions.**

Melissa is **in** the pool.

Tom is **at** the park.

These words are prepositions:

on **in** **under** **for** **to** **behind** **onto**

Look at the pictures. Finish each sentence.
Use a preposition from the box.

in **on** **down** **over**

1. The girl slides __________ the slide.
2. The children are __________ the sandbox.
3. The bird flies __________ the park.
4. The children play __________ the swings.

Prepositions in Sentences

Skills:
Write prepositions;
Use prepositions

Read the preposition. Read the sentence.
Write the preposition to finish the sentence.

1. **on** The children run __________ the grass.
2. **into** Justin crawls __________ the tunnel.
3. **under** Jenna reads a book __________ the tree.
4. **between** Javier stands __________ the gates.
5. **by** I will wait __________ the big tree.
6. **over** The sun shines __________ the park.

Skills:
Write periods after street abbreviations;
Form street abbreviations

Periods with Abbreviations of Street Names

You can make a street name shorter by using an abbreviation. Write a period (.) at the end of a street abbreviation.

Name	Abbreviation
Road	Rd.
Avenue	Ave.
Drive	Dr.
Highway	Hwy.
Circle	Cir.
Boulevard	Blvd.
Street	St.
Lane	Ln.
Court	Ct.

Read the sentence. Write a period after the abbreviation.

1. Jerome lives on Stay Ct___ near a park.

2. Stan waits on Apple Ln___ for the bus.

Read the sentence. Write the abbreviation of the underlined word. Use a period.

3. Bart lives on Harmony <u>Drive</u>. __________

4. Kristen works on Jones <u>Road</u>. __________

All in the Picture

Skill:
Use visual information to show understanding of prepositions

Look at the picture. Then answer the questions.

1. How many birds are **on** the trees? ______ birds

2. How many children are **near** the birds? ______ children

Look at the picture. Then answer the questions.

3. How many children are **on** the swings? ______ children

4. How many children go **down** the slide? ______ child or children

Skills:

Use visual information to show understanding of prepositions;

Write periods after street abbreviations

Write It Right!

Does the sentence tell what the picture shows?
Circle **yes** or **no**.

1 

The picnic table is on the food.

yes no

2 

The tree sits under the girl.

yes no

3 

The boy sits in the tire swing.

yes no

The abbreviation is missing a period. Fix the sentence.

4. Shell Blvd is where Toni lives.

5. Take Lemon Ave to get to the park.

6. The best park is on Leeds Rd by the school.

Street Signs

Look at the street signs. Answer the questions with abbreviations. Use periods.

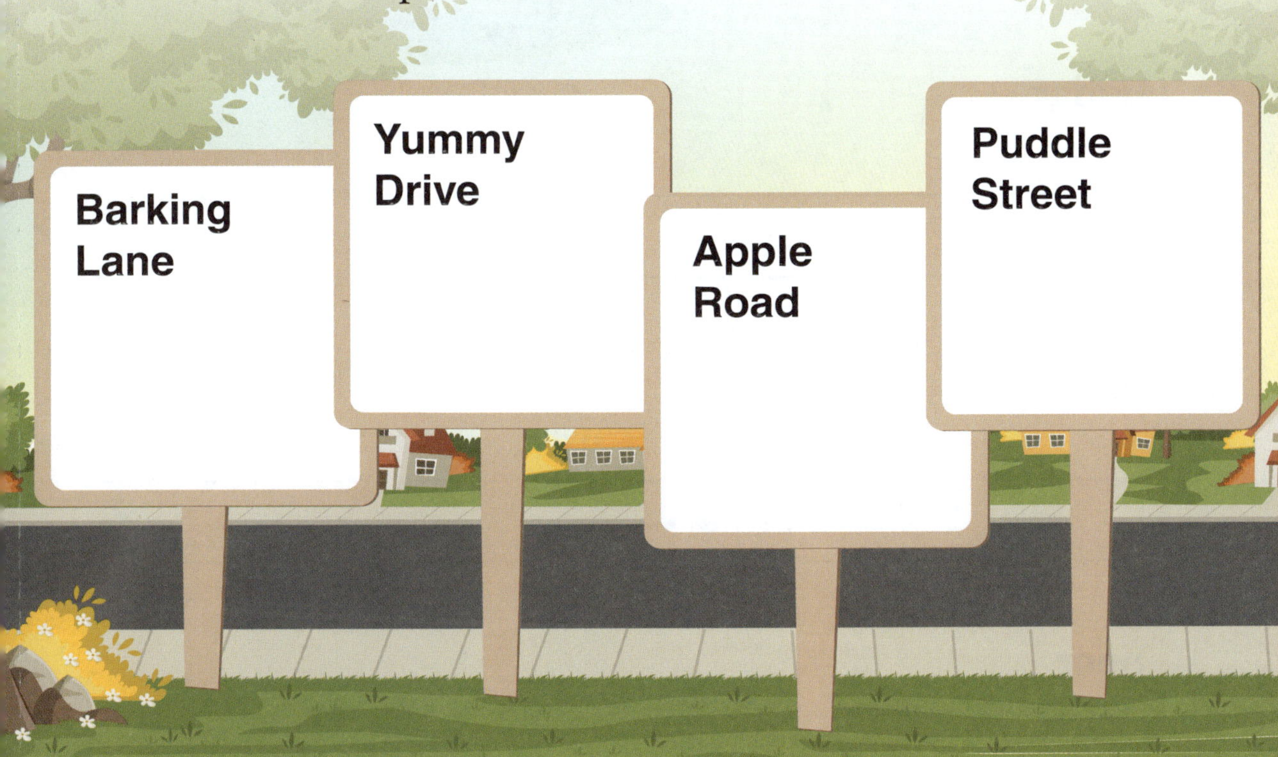

Skills:
Use visual information;
Write street abbreviations correctly using periods;
Use clues to answer questions;
Draw

1. Where do a lot of dogs live?

____

2. Where do a lot of trees grow?

____

3. Were does it rain a lot?

____

4. Where are there picnic tables?

____

5. The street signs need pictures. Draw a picture on each sign. Then color the signs and pictures.

Skills:
Produce sentences using prepositions;
Produce sentences using street abbreviations with correct punctuation

At the Park

Write a sentence about a park.
Use the word that tells **where**.

1. under

____

____

2. by

____

____

3. near

____

____

Write a sentence with a street name abbreviation.
Remember to use correct punctuation.

4. Write a sentence that tells the street you live on.

____

____

5. Write a sentence that tells the street your school is on.

____

____

Read the text.

Going to See the Dentist

When you visit the dentist, you must open your mouth to show the dentist your **teeth**. The dentist cleans people's teeth. **Men**, **women**, and **children** can go to the dentist. When **people** have teeth that hurt, the dentist can help. There are dentists all over the world. There are dentists in Tampa, Florida. And there are dentists in Rome, Italy. It's good to visit the dentist.

Read the rules. Answer the questions.

Grammar **Irregular plural nouns** are nouns that have special spellings to name more than one thing.

How many purple **irregular plural nouns** can you find in the text? _____

Punctuation In a sentence, a **comma** , goes between a city and a state or a city and a country.

How many orange **commas** between cities and states or countries can you find in the text? _____

Concepts:

Irregular plural nouns have specific spellings that do not follow a standard rule;

Commas separate the different elements of an address

Go and See

Skills:
Identify irregular plural nouns;
Match irregular plural nouns to their singular forms

Irregular Plural Nouns

Some nouns have special spellings to name **more than one**.

one mouse	two **mice**
one goose	two **geese**
one ox	two **oxen**
one wolf	two **wolves**

People like to see animals. Draw a line to match the word that names one to the word that names more than one.

1. goose •	• oxen
2. ox •	• wolves
3. mouse •	• geese
4. wolf •	• mice

Read the sentence. Circle the noun that has a special spelling to name more than one.

5. Children like to go to the zoo.

6. Can people feed an animal there?

7. The geese eat together.

Going to See the Lake

Skills:
Write irregular plural nouns;
Use irregular plural nouns;
Use visual information;
Distinguish between correct and incorrect forms of irregular plural nouns

Read the special nouns in the box. Write the best noun to finish the sentence. **HINT:** Some nouns have the same spelling for one and more than one.

sheep	deer	geese	fish

1. There are ____________ in the lake.
2. Young ____________ have spots on their fur.
3. Large ____________ fly over the lake.
4. Fluffy ____________ say "baa" near the lake.

Circle the correct words that tell about the picture.

5. 

two wolf
two wolves

6. 

three fishies
three fish

7. 

three sheep
three sheeps

Skill:
Write commas to separate the city from the state or the city from the country in an address

Commas Between City and State or City and Country

When you write an address, use a **comma** (,) between the city and the state.

350 Fifth Ave.
New York, NY 10118

In a sentence, use a comma between a city and state or a city and country.

There is an art museum in Dallas, Texas.
There is a lot to see in Beijing, China.

The sentence is missing a comma. Write the comma.

1. Disney World is in Orlando___ Florida.

2. There is a beautiful tower in Seoul___ South Korea.

3. You can take a plane to Cairo___ Egypt.

4. You can visit President Abraham Lincoln's old house in Springfield___ Illinois.

Going to the Market

Are the irregular plural nouns below shown in the picture? Circle **yes** or **no**. Then color the picture. HINT: Remember, **plural** means **more than one**. Circle **yes** if there is more than one.

women	yes	no	**mice**	yes	no
men	yes	no	**children**	yes	no
geese	yes	no	**feet**	yes	no

Skills:

Use visual information to show understanding of irregular plural nouns;

Recognize irregular plural nouns

Go and See

Skills:

Form irregular plural nouns;

Identify incorrect forms of irregular plural nouns;

Write commas to separate cities from countries

Write It Right!

Read the sentence. The irregular plural noun is wrong. Write it correctly on the line.

1. Mouses can be brown or white. ____________

2. Sheeps have wool that keeps them warm. ____________

3. Deers can be playful. ____________

The sentence is missing a comma. Write a comma to fix the sentence.

4. Lots of animals live near Halifax Canada.

5. There is an animal park in Nairobi Kenya.

6. You can see koalas in Brisbane Australia.

Let's Mail a Letter!

Write the commas on the envelope so it can be mailed.

1500 Cassie St.
Monterey CA 93940

Fun Land
1211 Fun Land Dr.
Anaheim CA 92802

Now write addresses on this envelope so it can be mailed. Remember to write commas.

____

____

____

____

Skills:

Write commas to separate cities from states in addresses;

Write complete addresses with correct punctuation

Go and See

Skills:

Write a complete address with correct punctuation;

Produce sentences with irregular plural nouns;

Use irregular plural nouns

A Letter to My Friend

Write a letter to your best friend. Put your address on the lines at the top of the page. Use the words in the word box in your letter.

children wolves geese mice

Concepts:
Verb tenses indicate the time of an action or state;
Abbreviations of month names end with a period

Read the story.

Winter, Spring, Summer, and Fall

Abbreviations

December = Dec.

April = Apr.

August = Aug.

October = Oct.

The weather changes. In December, it **snows**. It **snowed** all day yesterday. It **will snow** all day tomorrow, too. In April, it **rains** a lot. It **rained** on my birthday last year. I think it **will rain** on my birthday again. In August, the sun **shines**. It **feels** hot. In October, the air **will feel** cold.

Read the rules. Answer the questions.

Grammar **Verb tenses** tell when actions happen.

How many purple **verbs** can you find?
These verbs tell what happens now. _____

How many orange **verbs** can you find?
These tell what already happened. _____

How many blue **verbs** can you find?
These tell what will happen later.
Hint: These verbs have two words. _____

Punctuation We use a **period** after the name of a month when we make it shorter.

How many green **periods** can you find above? _____

Skills:

Write verbs in the present, past, and future tenses;

Use verbs in the present, past, and future tenses

Verb Tenses

A **verb** can tell about what is happening now, what already happened, or what will happen in the future.

Happening Now: Jonah **picks** a flower.

Already Happened: Jonah **picked** a flower.

Will Happen: Jonah **will pick** a flower.

Finish the sentence. Write the verb to tell what is happening now.

1. In the summer, Billy ____swims____ in the pool.

Finish the sentence. Write the verb to tell what already happened.

2. In the fall, Cooper ____kicked____ the ball.

Finish the sentence. Write the verb to tell what will happen.

3. Heidi ____will make____ shapes in the snow.

Verb Tense Practice

Skills:
Identify verb tenses;
Use verbs in the present, past, and future tenses;
Produce a sentence using a verb in the past tense

Finish the sentence with the verb that tells what is **happening now**.

1. Naomi ______________ pictures on a rainy day.
colored colors

Finish the sentence with the verb that tells what **already happened**.

2. The dog ______________ into the pile of leaves.
jumped will jump

Finish the sentence with the verb that tells what **will happen**.

3. Javier ______________ by the fire on a cold day.
sits will sit

Write a sentence. Tell about something you did in the fall.

4. ____

____

Skill:
Form abbreviations of month names with correct punctuation

Periods with Abbreviations of Months

Most months have an abbreviation. The abbreviation ends with a period.

May, **June**, and **July** are not abbreviated. Their names are already short.

Month	Abbreviation
January	Jan.
February	Feb.
March	Mar.
April	Apr.
August	Aug.
September	Sept.
October	Oct.
November	Nov.
December	Dec.

Write the abbreviation for the name of the month.
Use correct punctuation.

1. October ________
2. December ________
3. February ________
4. September ________
5. January ________
6. November ________
7. March ________
8. August ________
9. April ________

Look at What Happens!

Skills:
Produce sentences using verbs in the present, past, and future tenses;
Use visual information to produce sentences

Use the pictures to write a sentence.

1. Write a sentence to tell what is happening now. Use the verb **eats**.

____

____

____

2. Write a sentence to tell what already happened. Use the verb **pulled**.

____

____

____

3. Write a sentence to tell what will happen. Use the verb **will wear**.

____

____

____

Skills:

Write sentences using verbs in the present, past, and future tenses;

Form verbs in the present, past, and future tenses;

Write periods to correct abbreviations of month names

The Four Seasons

Write It Right!

Write the sentence so it tells what is **happening now.**

1. I will play in the snow.

____

____

Write the sentence so it tells what **already happened**.

2. I jump in the puddle.

____

____

Write the sentence so it tells what **will happen**.

3. I ride the bike.

____

____

Read the sentence. The abbreviation is missing a period. Write a period to fix it.

4. Piper likes Oct because she likes the weather.
5. Toya wears boots in Feb to keep her feet warm.
6. Yoshi has a party every Nov for his birthday.

Fun Months

Write a period after the abbreviation. Then draw a line to match the month to its abbreviation.

1. 
Jan •

• 
April

2. 
Apr •

• 
February

3. 
Oct •

• 
January

4. 

Feb •

• 
October

5. Write a word that tells about January. ____________________

6. Write a word that tells about April. ____________________

7. Write a word that tells about October. ____________________

8. Write a word that tells about February. ____________________

Skills:

Identify abbreviations of month names;

Write periods to correct abbreviations of month names;

Use visual information;

Match month names with their abbreviations

Skills:

Form verbs in the present, past, and future tenses;

Use verbs in the present, past, and future tenses;

Identify correct and incorrect punctuation of abbreviations of month names

Things We Like to Do

Use the verbs in the pencil to finish the sentences.

will build **jumped** **steps**

Write a verb that tells what is **happening now**.

1. Javier ______________ by the fire on a cold day.

Write a verb that tells what **already happened**.

2. Sheila ______________ in a pile of leaves.

Write a verb that tells what **will happen**.

3. Sheila ______________ a snowman.

Read the sentence. Does the month abbreviation have a period? Circle **yes** or **no**.

4. Apr 11 is my birthday. yes no

5. I went to school on Jan 2. yes no

6. On Oct. 3 I will go to a party. yes no

Read the story.

A Week with My Friends

On Sunday, I ate dinner at Sam's house. Sam said the noodles were good. Julie said the salad was **better**. All of us thought the pizza was the **best** of all. On Monday, we rode bikes. I fell and got a bad scrape. Sam bumped his elbow and got a **worse** scrape. But Julie got the **worst** scrape on her toe. On Thursday, we walked with our dogs. Julie's dog is **smaller** than mine. Sam's dog is the **smallest** of all. I hope next week will be fun, too!

Abbreviations

Sunday = Sun.

Monday = Mon.

Thursday = Thurs.

Read the rules. Answer the questions.

Grammar Some special **adjectives** tell how two or more nouns are different. These adjectives compare.

How many green comparing **adjectives** can you find in the story? _____

Punctuation We can make the names of the days of the week shorter by using abbreviations. The abbreviations end with a **period** (.).

How many orange **periods with abbreviations of weekdays** can you find above? _____

Concepts:

Comparative adjectives compare two nouns, and superlative adjectives compare three or more nouns;

An abbreviation of a day of the week ends with a period

With My Friends

Skills:

Correctly use comparative and superlative adjectives;

Write comparative and superlative adjectives;

Show understanding of comparative and superlative adjectives

Comparative and Superlative Adjectives

Adjectives that end with **-er** tell how two nouns are different.

Felix is **shorter** than Nicole.

Adjectives that end with **-est** tell how more than two nouns are different.

Nicole is short, Felix is shorter, and Darren is the **shortest** of all.

Read the sentence. Write the correct adjective on the line.

1. Sina is ____________ than Cole.
   tall   taller

2. Toya is the ____________ of all her friends.
   taller   tallest

3. Janet has ____________ hair than Eddie.
   dark   darker

4. Dale has the ____________ hair of all.
   dark   darkest

Write the name of a friend you have who is faster than you.

5. ____________

Write the name of your funniest friend.

6. ____________

Friends Eating Fruit

The adjectives **good** and **bad** tell about nouns. The adjectives **better** and **worse** tell how two nouns are different. The adjectives **best** and **worst** tell how three or more nouns are different.

The cherry is **good**. The mango is **better** than the cherry. The peach is the **best** of all the fruits.

This lemon is **bad**. That orange is **worse** than this lemon. The melon is the **worst** of all of these fruits.

Skills:
Correctly use comparative and superlative adjectives;
Write comparative and superlative adjectives

Write the correct adjective from the box to finish the sentence. Use each adjective once.

best	good	better

1. Janis ate a ____________ plum.
2. Joe's plum was ____________ than Janis's plum.
3. Gene's plum was the ____________ of all the plums.

worst	bad	worse

4. Callie ate a ____________ grape.
5. Marta ate a ____________ grape than Callie's.
6. Tyrone's grape was the ____________ of all.

Skill:
Form abbreviations of days of the week using correct punctuation

Periods with Abbreviations of Days of the Week

Each day of the week has an abbreviation.
The abbreviation ends with a **period** (.).

Day of the Week	Abbreviation
Sunday	Sun.
Monday	Mon.
Tuesday	Tues.
Wednesday	Wed.
Thursday	Thurs.
Friday	Fri.
Saturday	Sat.

Write an abbreviation to answer the question.

1. What is the first day of the week? ________
2. What is the last day of the week? ________
3. What is the day before Thursday? ________
4. Which day of the week comes after Sunday? ________
5. Which day of the week comes before Friday? ________

All About My Friends

Skills:
Show understanding of comparative and superlative adjectives;
Draw

Read the questions. Then draw a picture of you and your friends. Last, answer the questions.

1. Who is the tallest? ____________________
2. Who is the shortest? ____________________
3. Who is the youngest? ____________________
4. Who is the oldest? ____________________
5. Who is shorter than you? ____________________
6. Who is taller than you? ____________________

Application

Skills:

Identify incorrect use of comparative and superlative adjectives;

Identify incorrect forms of comparative and superlative adjectives;

Form abbreviations of days of the week using correct punctuation

Write It Right!

The adjective in the sentence is wrong. It is underlined. Write the correct adjective on the line.

1. Kate is tallest than Paula. ____________

2. Earl has the worse flu of all his friends. ____________

3. Leah thinks Tony's house is gooder than Amy's house. ____________

4. Dom is the faster of all. ____________

Circle the day of the week in each sentence. Write the abbreviation on the line.

5. On Tuesday my friend is coming over. ________

6. Every Friday Joe eats dinner with us. ________

7. On Saturday I will sleep over at my friend's house. ________

One School Week

Skills:
Use visual information to answer questions;
Form abbreviations of days of the week using correct punctuation

Read the notes on the classroom's board. Then answer the questions. Use the abbreviation for the day of the week, and use a period.

1. What day is the school play? ________
2. What day is Shelly's birthday? ________
3. What day is P.E. Day? ________
4. What day is Music Day? ________

Skills:

Show understanding of comparative and superlative adjectives;

Produce sentences with abbreviations of days of the week;

Form abbreviations of days of the week using correct punctuation

Funny Friends

Answer the items.

1. Write the name of someone you know who is funnier than a clown. ____________________

2. Write one thing that is taller than your best friend. ____________________

3. Write the fastest animal you know. ____________________

Write 3 sentences. In each sentence write one thing you do on a day of the week. Use an abbreviation for the day of the week. Remember to use a period.

4. ____

____

____

5. ____

____

____

6. ____

____

____

Concepts:
Articles precede nouns;
Commas set apart the words *yes* and *no* in sentences

Read the text.

What About Bugs?

Do you think some bugs look scary? Yes, bugs can make some people feel afraid. But some bugs look pretty. There are many different kinds of bugs. Have you ever seen **a** beetle? Yes, **the** picture shows **a** beetle. It is **a** large bug. Do you think all beetles are **the** same? No, they are not. What bugs have you seen? You have probably seen **an** ant before. Ants and other bugs are important. Do you know why? Yes, they help keep **the** planet clean and green!

Read the rules. Answer the questions.

Grammar We use the words **a**, **an**, and **the** before nouns.

How many green words can you find in the text?

a _____ **an** _____ **the** _____

Punctuation We use a **comma** after the words **yes** and **no** in a sentence.

How many **commas** can you find after **yes** and **no** in the text? _____

Bugs and Insects

Skills:
Write articles;
Use articles correctly

Articles

We use the words **a** and **an** before words that name one person, place, animal, or thing. Use **an** for words that begin with **a**, **e**, **i**, **o**, or **u**.

A worm has no legs. **An** ant has six legs.

We can use the word **the** before singular and plural naming words. Mostly we use **the** to tell about a special person or thing.

The bee buzzes. **The** insect flies. **The** ants work.

Finish the sentence. Write **a** or **an** before a word that names one. Write **the** before a word that names one or more than one.

1. A fruit worm eats ______ apple.
2. The grasshoppers will eat ______ plants.
3. A bee gets food from ______ flower.

4. A tick gets food from ______ animal.
5. A moth is ______ insect that gets food from plants.
6. Flies land on ______ bits of food they find.

Buggy Words

Skills:
Write articles;
Use articles correctly

Write **a** or **an** before words that name one. Write **the** before words that name one or more than one.

1. ______ termites

2. ______ wasp

3. ______ ant

4. ______ fly

5. ______ earwig

6. ______ beetles

Skill:
Write commas to set apart the words *yes* and *no* in sentences

Commas with Yes and No

Some sentences answer a question with **yes** or **no**.
Use a **comma** after the words **yes** and **no** in a sentence.

Yes, that is a grasshopper.

No, that is not a termite.

Read the sentence. Then write a comma after **yes** or **no**.

1. No a fly is not a beetle.
2. Yes some beetles are black.
3. Yes crickets can chirp.
4. No honeybees do not live in a house.
5. Yes wasps can sting.
6. Yes caterpillars can crawl.
7. Yes moths have wings.

Make a Bug

Look at the word in the box. Draw to make the word look like a bug. Then write a sentence about the bug you drew. Use **a**, **an**, or **the** in your sentence.

Example

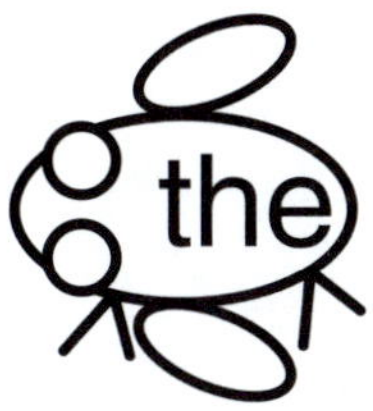

The fly goes up.

1. a

2. an

3. the

Skills:
Produce sentences with articles;
Use articles correctly;
Draw

Bugs and Insects

Application

Skills:

Identify incorrect use of articles;

Write articles correctly;

Correctly use commas to set apart the words *yes* and *no* in sentences

Write It Right!

The sentence has a word that is wrong. It is underlined. Write the correct word on the line. Use a capital letter.

1. An grasshopper can jump. ________

2. A bees that make honey work hard. ________

3. A ant can carry food. ________

The sentence is missing a comma after **yes** or **no**. Write the comma in the sentence.

4. Yes some bugs can bite.

5. No worms do not have arms, legs, or eyes.

6. Yes butterflies have colors on their wings.

Which Bugs Have You Seen?

Look at the picture. Write a sentence to answer the question. Write the word **yes** or **no**, and remember to use a comma.

1 Have you seen one of these bugs before?

____

____

2 Have you seen one of these bugs before?

____

____

3 Have you seen one of these bugs before?

____

____

Skills:

Produce sentences using commas correctly;

Use commas to set apart the words *yes* and *no* in sentences;

Use visual information to answer questions

Bugs and Insects

Skills:

Produce sentences with articles;

Use articles correctly;

Produce sentences using commas to set apart the words *yes* and *no*

Bugs, Bugs, Everywhere!

Write a sentence. Use a word from the word box.
Use **a**, **an**, or **the** in your sentence.

bees	worm	ant

1. ____

____

2. ____

____

3. ____

____

Write a sentence to answer the question.
Write the word **yes** or **no** in the sentence.
Remember to use a comma.

4. Do you like bugs?

____

____

5. Would you pick up a caterpillar?

____

____

Concepts:
Avoid using double negatives in writing;
Sentences begin with capital letters

Read the text.

People's Pets

There are many kinds of pets. Some people have dogs or cats. You can even have a bird or a snake. Can you think of some other pets? Some people do **not** have pets, and that is okay, too. People who have pets need to give them food, water, and care. A pet can get sick if it **never** gets food or water. You can also buy toys for your pet. There is a lot to learn about pets!

Read the rules. Answer the questions.

Grammar We do not use two of these words together in the same sentence:

no not never nothing nobody

When two of the purple words are together in a sentence, the sentence is incorrect.

How many purple **words** can you find in the text? _____

Find It!

Punctuation Write a **capital letter** at the beginning of a sentence.

How many **capital letters** at the beginning of a sentence can you find in the text? _____

Pets People Have

Skills:
Identify double negatives;
Correct sentences with double negatives;
Avoid using double negatives

Double Negatives

We never use two of these words in the same sentence:

no **not** **never** **nothing** **nobody**

Wrong: Pets do **not** know **nothing** about math.
Correct: Pets do **not** know anything about math.
Correct: Pets know **nothing** about math.

Read the sentences. Circle the sentence that is correct.

1. Dogs never do not drink tea. Dogs do not drink tea.
2. Cats never should not eat nuts. Cats should never eat nuts.
3. Fish have no legs. Fish do not have no legs.
4. Snakes do not have no fur. Snakes do not have fur.
5. Rats do not read. Rats do not read nothing.

Finish the sentence.

6. Fish do not ______________________________.

Do the Words Go Together?

Skill:
Identify sentences with double negatives

Read the sentence. Do all the words belong together in the sentence? Circle **yes** or **no**.

1. Hamsters are not never the same as cats. yes no
2. Cats do not sleep all day. yes no
3. Fish never do nothing out of water. yes no
4. Some people do not have no cats or dogs. yes no
5. A bunny does not have purple fur. yes no
6. Hamsters have no wings. yes no
7. Snakes are not no cuddly pets. yes no
8. Frogs are not furry. yes no

Skill:
Use correct capitalization in sentences

Mechanics: Capital Letters in Sentences

All sentences begin with a **capital letter**.

Telling sentence: **A** dog has a tail.

Asking sentence: **D**o bunnies have tails?

Write the correct word to finish the sentence.

1. ____________ pets like to play with people.
   Some   some

2. ____________ can have dreams.
   dogs   Dogs

3. ____________ can see well in the dark.
   Cats   cats

4. ____________ take a lot of naps.
   bunnies   Bunnies

5. ____________ fish can smell things.
   Many   many

Note for the Dog Walker

Read the note. It tells how to take care of a dog.
In each sentence, cross out the word that doesn't belong.

Instructions For Dog Walker

1. You should not never let the dog off its leash.
2. You can never not leave the dog alone for 8 hours.
3. The dog should not eat nothing at the table.
4. The dog should not have no juice.

Skills:

Identify double negatives;

Correct sentences with double negatives;

Draw

Draw a picture of a person walking a dog.

Skills:
Identify double negatives;
Identify capitalization errors

Write It Right!

Read the sentence. It has words that do not belong together. Circle the two words that should not be in the same sentence.

1. It's not safe for nobody to have a tiger as a pet.

2. Fish can never not play out of water.

3. Hamsters do not like to share no food with other hamsters.

Read the sentence. Circle the words that should not have a capital letter. Underline the words that need a capital letter.

4. some people have a Pet monkey.

5. pets can come in different Sizes.

6. special animal doctors help us Take care of our pets.

What Comes First?

Look at the animals in the picture. Then finish the sentence. Use a capital letter.

1. ______________ have long ears.

2. ______________ like to take naps.

3. ______________ sing songs sometimes.

Draw a picture of an animal you like.
Then write a sentence about the animal you drew.

4. ______________________________

____

____

5. ______________________________

____

____

Skills:

Use correct capitalization in sentences;

Draw;

Produce sentences using correct capitalization

Pets People Have

Skills:

Produce sentences using correct capitalization;

Identify double negatives;

Avoid using double negatives;

Write sentences to correct double negatives

Pets Are Fun to Write About

Read the question. Write a sentence to answer the question. Use a capital letter.

1. What pet do you wish you had?

2. What is one thing you can do to take care of a pet?

3. What is a pet you do not want to have?

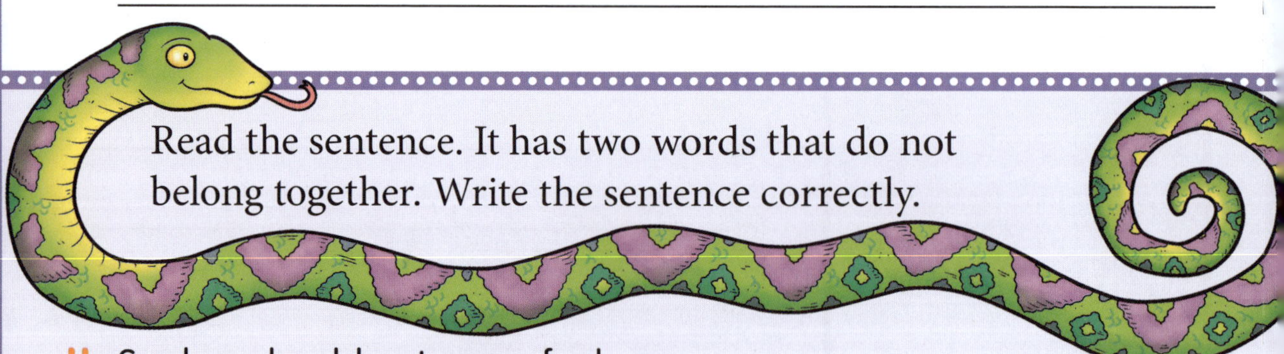

Read the sentence. It has two words that do not belong together. Write the sentence correctly.

4. Snakes should not never feel warm.

5. Snakes never have no hair.

Language Handbook

Remove this handbook and staple it together. Use it to remember grammar and punctuation rules.

Grammar

Nouns	
A **common noun** names a person, place, animal, or thing.	teacher park dog cup The **cow** eats **grass**.
A **proper noun** is a special name. It begins with a capital letter.	Elliot July Anna **Miss Doe** visited us on **Saturday**.
A **singular noun** names one person, place, animal, or thing. A **plural noun** names more than one. Add **s** or **es** to make nouns plural. For nouns that end in **-y**, change **y** to **i** and add **es**.	lady rock box pony The **lady** eats a **plum**. ladies rocks boxes ponies The **ladies** eat **plums**.
A **possessive noun** shows that something belongs to someone or something. It has an apostrophe.	Erin's cat the girl's bowl The **tree's** trunk is brown.
An **irregular plural noun** names more than one thing and has a special spelling. Try to remember how to spell irregular plural nouns.	goose = geese mouse = mice The **geese** fly away.

Adjectives	
An **adjective** tells more about a noun.	**red** **soft** **stinky** **sweet** **loud** The pen is **long**.
Some special adjectives **compare two nouns**. They tell how two nouns are different.	**taller** **bigger** **better** **worse** Jay is **taller** than Mac.
Other special adjectives **compare three or more nouns**.	**tallest** **biggest** **best** **worst** Mac is tall, Jay is taller, but Amy is the **tallest** of all.
Use the word **an** before nouns that name one and begin with **a**, **e**, **i**, **o**, or **u**. Use **a** before other nouns that name one. Use the word **the** before any noun.	**an** **a** **the** **An** ant is small. **A** bear is big. **The** cow is brown. **The** cows are big.

Verbs	
A **verb** tells what a noun is or does.	**run** **draw** **is** **seems** **feels** The fruit **tastes** fresh.
A **singular verb** tells what one noun does.	**Dina plays.** **The girl reads.** The boy **runs**.
A **plural verb** tells what more than one noun does.	**Dina and Ed play.** **The girls read.** The boys **run**.
Verb tenses show when an action happens.	**is happening now:** Joe **plays**. **already happened:** Joe **played**. **will happen:** Joe **will play**.

Pronouns

A **pronoun** can take the place of a noun in a sentence.	**I** **me** **you** **he** **him** **she** **her** **it** **we** **us** **they** **them** **She** gave the paper to **them**.

Sentences

All sentences have a **naming part** and a **telling part**.	The **naming part** of a sentence is the part before the verb. **The desk** has a sticker on it. The **telling part** of a sentence is the verb and everything that comes after it. The desk **has a sticker on it**.

Prepositions

A **preposition** tells where a noun is. It joins a noun to another noun in the sentence.	**on** **over** **across** **by** **onto** **off** The dog ran **across** the road.

Usage

Do not use two of these words in the same sentence: **no**, **not**, **never**, **nothing**, **nobody**.	**wrong:** Pam **never** had **no** milk. **right:** Pam **never** had milk. **right:** Pam had **no** milk.

Punctuation

Periods ◯	
Use a **period** ◯ at the end of a sentence that tells something.	Apples are good.
Use a **period** ◯ after some titles before a name.	Mrs. Mr. Dr. Mr. Lam is my teacher.
Use a **period** ◯ after the abbreviation of the name of a street.	Street = St. Lane = Ln. Road = Rd. The house on Leaf St. is big.
Use a **period** ◯ after the abbreviation of the name of a month.	January = Jan. August = Aug. School begins on Aug. 7 this year.
Use a **period** ◯ after the abbreviation of the name of a day of the week.	Tuesday = Tues. Saturday = Sat. Every Tues. and Thurs. we have a picnic.

Question Marks ?	
Use a question mark ? at the end of a sentence that asks a question.	Do you like bananas?

Exclamation Points !	
Use an **exclamation point** ! at the end of a sentence that tells something with strong feeling or excitement.	I can't wait to go to the park!

Apostrophes ’

Use an **apostrophe** ’ in a contraction, or a word made of two words.	I am ⟶ I’m you have ⟶ you’ve I’m at school.
Use an **apostrophe** ’ in a possessive noun, or a noun that shows that something belongs to someone or something.	Megan’s shoe the girls’ pencils The tree’s trunk is bumpy.

Colons :

Use a **colon** : between the hour and minutes in the time.	8:00 4:15 10:30 12:45 Bailey woke up at 7:30.

Commas ,

Use a **comma** , after the greeting and closing of a letter.	Dear Mom, — **greeting** Thank you for the lunch you made for me. I liked it a lot. Love, Zelda — **closing**
Use a **comma** , in a date between the day and the year.	July 24, 2019 December 5, 2020 The party is on August 4, 2020.
Use a **comma** , between each word in a list in a sentence and before the word **and** in a list.	We eat bread, grapes, and cheese. Today I played, rested, and ate.

Commas , *continued*

Use a comma in an **address** between the city and state or the city and country.	421 Apple Rd. Bing City**,** IL 60174
Use a comma in a **sentence** between the city and state or the city and country.	I was born in Provo**,** Utah. You visited Hue**,** Vietnam.
Use a comma after the word **yes** or **no** in a sentence.	Yes**,** it is sunny outside. No**,** it did not rain today.

Titles of Books and Movies

Underline the titles of books and movies.	Meena reads **The Little Prince**. Nat saw **Toy Story**.

Capital Letters (Mechanics)

Use a **capital letter** at the beginning of a sentence.	**T**he fly is buzzing in my ear. **D**ogs bark at lots of things.

Answer Key

To download a larger version of this answer key, go to: ***www.evan-moor.com/resources***
Enter your email address and this resource code: **EMC9951**

Page 5

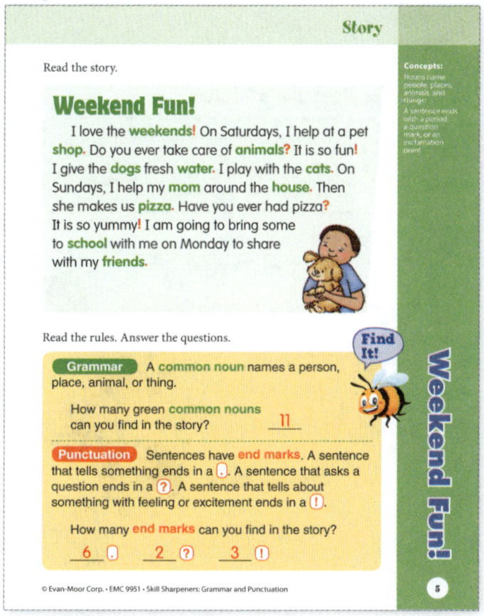

Story

Read the story.

Weekend Fun!

I love the weekends! On Saturdays, I help at a pet shop. Do you ever take care of animals? It is so fun! I give the dogs fresh water. I play with the cats. On Sundays, I help my mom around the house. Then she makes us pizza. Have you ever had pizza? It is so yummy! I am going to bring some to school with me on Monday to share with my friends.

Read the rules. Answer the questions.

Grammar: A common noun names a person, place, animal, or thing.

How many green common nouns can you find in the story? 11

Punctuation: Sentences have end marks. A sentence that tells something ends in a (.). A sentence that asks a question ends in a (?). A sentence that tells about something with feeling or excitement ends in a (!).

How many end marks can you find in the story? 6 (.) 2 (?) 3 (!)

Weekend Fun!

Page 6

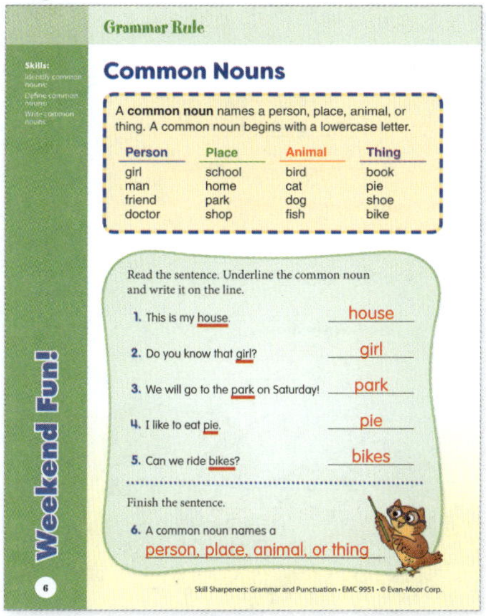

Grammar Rule

Common Nouns

A **common noun** names a person, place, animal, or thing. A common noun begins with a lowercase letter.

Person	Place	Animal	Thing
girl	school	bird	book
man	home	cat	pie
friend	park	dog	shoe
doctor	shop	fish	bike

Read the sentence. Underline the common noun and write it on the line.

1. This is my house. house
2. Do you know that girl? girl
3. We will go to the park on Saturday! park
4. I like to eat pie. pie
5. Can we ride bikes? bikes

Finish the sentence.

6. A common noun names a person, place, animal, or thing

Page 7

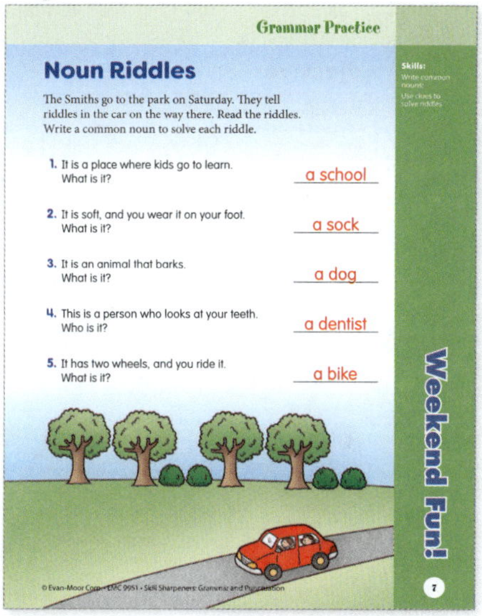

Grammar Practice

Noun Riddles

The Smiths go to the park on Saturday. They tell riddles in the car on the way there. Read the riddles. Write a common noun to solve each riddle.

1. It is a place where kids go to learn. What is it? a school
2. It is soft, and you wear it on your foot. What is it? a sock
3. It is an animal that barks. What is it? a dog
4. This is a person who looks at your teeth. Who is it? a dentist
5. It has two wheels, and you ride it. What is it? a bike

Page 8

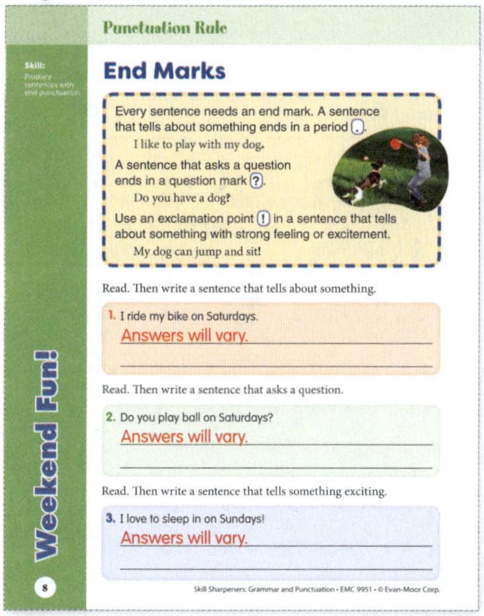

Punctuation Rule

End Marks

Every sentence needs an end mark. A sentence that tells about something ends in a period (.).
I like to play with my dog.
A sentence that asks a question ends in a question mark (?).
Do you have a dog?
Use an exclamation point (!) in a sentence that tells about something with strong feeling or excitement.
My dog can jump and sit!

Read. Then write a sentence that tells about something.
1. I ride my bike on Saturdays.
Answers will vary.

Read. Then write a sentence that asks a question.
2. Do you play ball on Saturdays?
Answers will vary.

Read. Then write a sentence that tells something exciting.
3. I love to sleep in on Sundays!
Answers will vary.

Page 9

Grammar Fun

Saturday at the Pet Shop

Help the boy get to the pet shop. Color only the boxes with nouns. REMEMBER A noun names a person, place, animal, or thing.

milk	go	sit
cat	sock	park
new	big	frog
book	apple	home
bike	pizza	sad
not	school	dog
feel	happy	pen

PET SHOP

Page 10

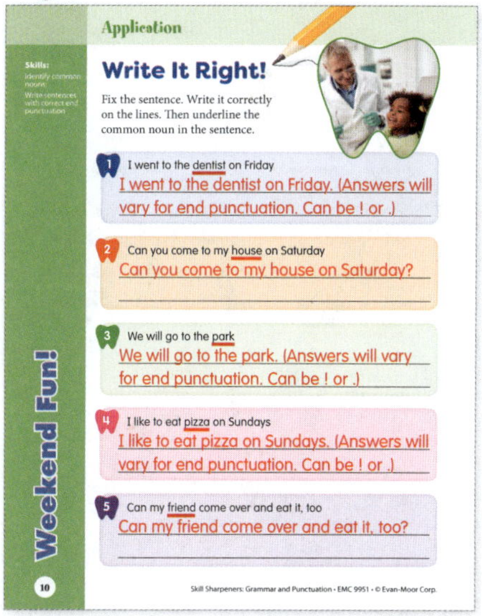

Application

Write It Right!

Fix the sentence. Write it correctly on the lines. Then underline the common noun in the sentence.

1. I went to the dentist on Friday
I went to the dentist on Friday. (Answers will vary for end punctuation. Can be ! or .)
2. Can you come to my house on Saturday
Can you come to my house on Saturday?
3. We will go to the park
We will go to the park. (Answers will vary for end punctuation. Can be ! or .)
4. I like to eat pizza on Sundays
I like to eat pizza on Sundays. (Answers will vary for end punctuation. Can be ! or .)
5. Can my friend come over and eat it, too
Can my friend come over and eat it, too?

Page 11

Punctuation Fun

Punctuation Match

Draw lines to match the sentences that have the same end marks.

1. Is that a mouse on a bike? — Is that a frog on the slide?
2. My dog has my sock! — I like ice cream!
3. I see two cakes. — There is an owl on my house.

Page 12

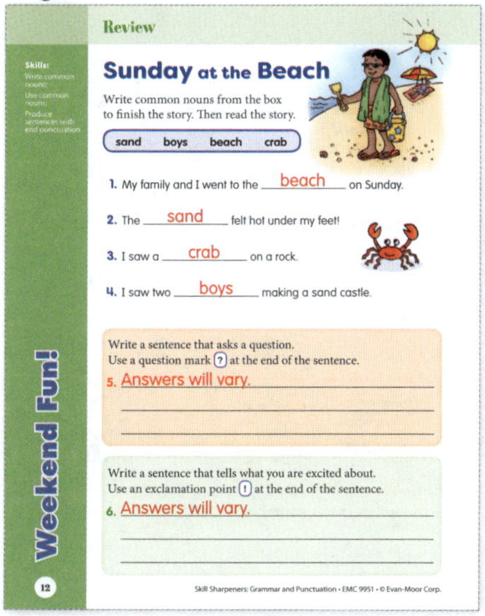

Review

Sunday at the Beach

Write common nouns from the box to finish the story. Then read the story.

sand boys beach crab

1. My family and I went to the beach on Sunday.
2. The sand felt hot under my feet!
3. I saw a crab on a rock.
4. I saw two boys making a sand castle.

Write a sentence that asks a question. Use a question mark (?) at the end of the sentence.
5. Answers will vary.

Write a sentence that tells what you are excited about. Use an exclamation point (!) at the end of the sentence.
6. Answers will vary.

Page 13

Story

Read the story.

A Day at the Farm

I am at Mr. Jim's farm with my class. The farm is fun! I see Miss Toro feeding some little ducks. I see a big horse. I see spotted cows eat grass. The ducks like the cold water. I hear the animals make loud noises. I pet the tall horse. Her hair is soft. Mr. Jim brushes the horse's hair. I smell something sweet coming from the small shop near the barn. Mrs. Jane made us a pie. I taste the sweet apples! Yum!

Read the rules. Answer the questions.

Grammar: An adjective tells more about something or someone. The word big is an adjective.

How many adjectives can you find in the story? 10

Punctuation: Some people have a title before their name. For example: Mrs. Lee. The title ends with a period (.).

How many orange periods after titles can you find? 3

The Five Senses

To download a larger version of this answer key, go to: ***www.evan-moor.com/resources***
Enter your email address and this resource code: **EMC9951**

Page 14

Grammar Rule

Adjectives

An **adjective** tells about a noun.
Adjectives can tell about size, shape, color, smell, taste, sound, number, and how something feels.
The mouse is **tiny**.
The cake smells **good**.

Look at the picture. Read the words.
Fill in the circle next to the adjective.

1. ○ kitten ● little
2. ● three ○ children
3. ● hot ○ sun
4. ○ candy ● sweet

The Five Senses

14 Skill Sharpeners: Grammar and Punctuation • EMC 9951 • © Evan-Moor Corp.

Page 15

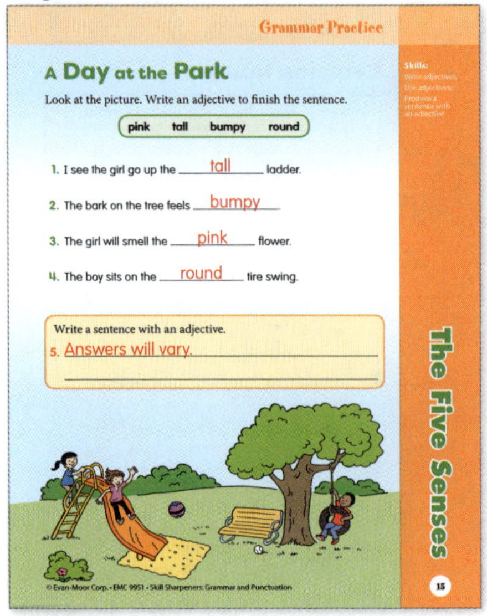
Grammar Practice

A Day at the Park

Look at the picture. Write an adjective to finish the sentence.

pink tall bumpy round

1. I see the girl go up the tall ladder.
2. The bark on the tree feels bumpy.
3. The girl will smell the pink flower.
4. The boy sits on the round tire swing.

Write a sentence with an adjective.
5. Answers will vary.

The Five Senses

© Evan-Moor Corp. • EMC 9951 • Skill Sharpeners: Grammar and Punctuation 15

Page 16

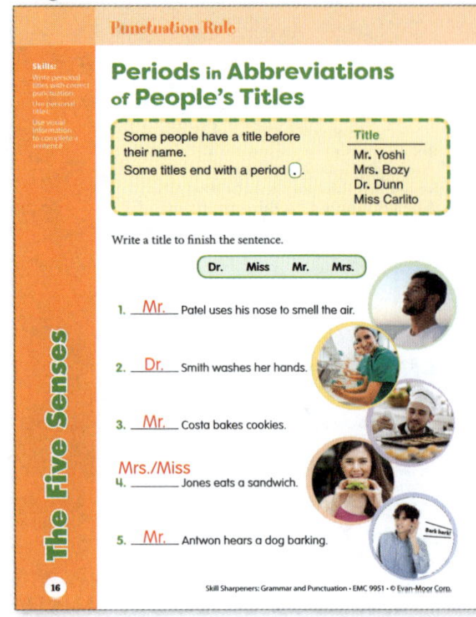
Punctuation Rule

Periods in Abbreviations of People's Titles

Some people have a title before their name.
Some titles end with a period (.).

Title
Mr. Yoshi
Mrs. Bozy
Dr. Dunn
Miss Carlito

Write a title to finish the sentence.

Dr. Miss Mr. Mrs.

1. Mr. Patel uses his nose to smell the air.
2. Dr. Smith washes her hands.
3. Mr. Costa bakes cookies.
4. Mrs./Miss Jones eats a sandwich.
5. Mr. Antwon hears a dog barking.

The Five Senses

16 Skill Sharpeners: Grammar and Punctuation • EMC 9951 • © Evan-Moor Corp.

Page 17

Grammar Fun

Using Our Senses!

Write an adjective from the word box to finish the sentence.

See: yellow green
1. The light is yellow.
2. I see the green frog.

Hear: loud quiet
3. The dog's bark is loud.
4. The mouse's footstep is very quiet.

Feel: cold soft
5. The ice cream feels cold.
6. This rabbit feels soft.

Smell: sweet stinky
7. The trash can smells stinky.
8. The pie smells sweet.

The Five Senses

© Evan-Moor Corp. • EMC 9951 • Skill Sharpeners: Grammar and Punctuation 17

Page 18

Application

Write It Right!

The adjective is in the wrong place in the sentence.
The noun is in the wrong place in the sentence.
Write the sentence to make it correct.

1. The tall is girl.
The girl is tall.
2. The white is milk.
The milk is white.
3. The good taste nuts.
The nuts taste good.

A period is missing in the sentence.
Write the sentence to make it correct.

4. Mr Smith feels cold.
Mr. Smith feels cold.
5. Dr Cam sees a sick person.
Dr. Cam sees a sick person.
6. Mrs Jenner looks friendly.
Mrs. Jenner looks friendly.

The Five Senses

18 Skill Sharpeners: Grammar and Punctuation • EMC 9951 • © Evan-Moor Corp.

Page 19

Punctuation Fun

A Picture That Needs a Title!

Look at the picture. Finish the sentences about the picture.
Write a title from the word box.

Mrs. Mr. Dr.

1. Mrs. Landis feels sick. Her head feels hot.
2. Dr. Nam helps Mrs. Landis to feel better.
3. Mr. Tyson waits for Mrs. Landis. He is her friend.
4. Mrs. Shore also waits. She feels sick, too.
5. Mrs. Shore wants Dr. Nam to help her feel better, too.

The Five Senses

© Evan-Moor Corp. • EMC 9951 • Skill Sharpeners: Grammar and Punctuation 19

Page 20

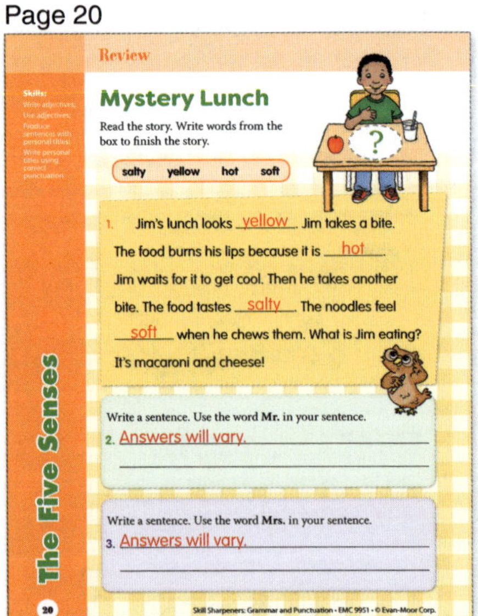
Review

Mystery Lunch

Read the story. Write words from the box to finish the story.

salty yellow hot soft

1. Jim's lunch looks yellow. Jim takes a bite. The food burns his lips because it is hot. Jim waits for it to get cool. Then he takes another bite. The food tastes salty. The noodles feel soft when he chews them. What is Jim eating? It's macaroni and cheese!

Write a sentence. Use the word **Mr.** in your sentence.
2. Answers will vary.

Write a sentence. Use the word **Mrs.** in your sentence.
3. Answers will vary.

The Five Senses

20 Skill Sharpeners: Grammar and Punctuation • EMC 9951 • © Evan-Moor Corp.

Page 21

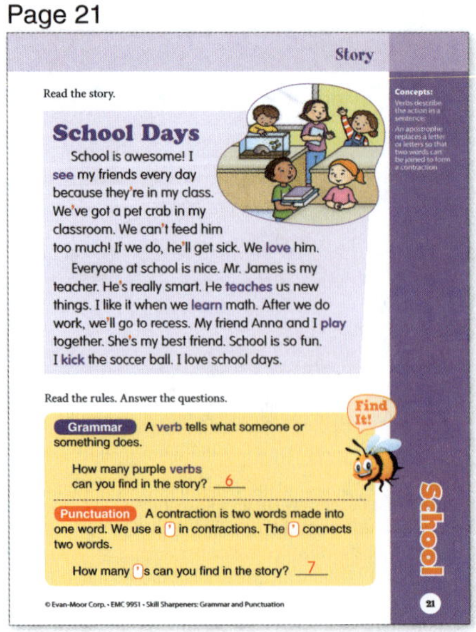
Story

Read the story.

School Days

School is awesome! I see my friends every day because they're in my class. We've got a pet crab in my classroom. We can't feed him too much! If we do, he'll get sick. We love him.

Everyone at school is nice. Mr. James is my teacher. He's really smart. He teaches us new things. I like it when we learn math. After we do work, we'll go to recess. My friend Anna and I play together. She's my best friend. School is so fun. I kick the soccer ball. I love school days.

Read the rules. Answer the questions.

Grammar A verb tells what someone or something does.
How many purple verbs can you find in the story? 6

Punctuation A contraction is two words made into one word. We use a ' in contractions. The ' connects two words.
How many 's can you find in the story? 7

Find It!

School

© Evan-Moor Corp. • EMC 9951 • Skill Sharpeners: Grammar and Punctuation 21

Page 22

Grammar Rule

Verbs

A **verb** is an action word.
A verb tells what someone or something does.
The teacher **adds** numbers.
The student **asks** a question.
The kids **play** kickball.

Read the sentence. Underline the action word.

1. The children sing songs.
2. James reads a book.
3. The teacher writes a note.
4. Dylan sits at his desk.
5. Sarah uses the blocks.
6. Debbie draws a picture.
7. The children talk in line.
8. Chelsea plays a math game.

School

22 Skill Sharpeners: Grammar and Punctuation • EMC 9951 • © Evan-Moor Corp.

To download a larger version of this answer key, go to: ***www.evan-moor.com/resources***
Enter your email address and this resource code: **EMC9951**

Page 23

Grammar Practice

After School

Look at the picture. Finish the sentence with a verb from the pencil.

rides play throws write sits eat

1. Jane sits in a chair.
2. Eduardo rides his bike to school.
3. The boys eat their food.
4. Dan throws the ball to Aaron.

Skills: Write verbs; Use verbs

School 23

© Evan-Moor Corp. • EMC 9951 • Skill Sharpeners: Grammar and Punctuation

Page 24

Punctuation Rule

Apostrophes in Contractions

A contraction is two words made into one word.
An apostrophe (') takes the place of the missing letters.
was not ⟶ was n̶o̶t ⟶ wasn't
can not ⟶ can n̶o̶t ⟶ can't

Draw a line to match the words to the contraction. Trace the apostrophe.

1. did not — didn't
2. are not — aren't
3. he is — he's
4. I am — I'm

Read the sentence. Circle the contraction.
5. (She's) having fun on a swing.

School 24

Skill Sharpeners: Grammar and Punctuation • EMC 9951 • © Evan-Moor Corp.

Page 25

Grammar Fun

The Verbs on the Bus

Help the buses get to school. Color only the windows that have verbs. A bus must have all its windows colored to get to school.

SCHOOL BUS A: read run dig smile
SCHOOL BUS B: small write big hop
SCHOOL BUS C: jump catch play draw

Which buses made it to school? Circle the letters. (A) B (C)

Skill: Identify verbs

School 25

© Evan-Moor Corp. • EMC 9951 • Skill Sharpeners: Grammar and Punctuation

Page 26

Application

Write It Right!

The verb is in the wrong place in the sentence. Write the sentence to make it correct.

EXAMPLE: Wrong: Pat on the floor **sits**. Right: Pat **sits** on the floor.

1. Jimmy the book reads. Jimmy reads the book.
2. Tracy her hand up puts. Tracy puts her hand up.
3. Abe and Sherry books carry. Abe and Sherry carry books.

An apostrophe is missing in each sentence. Write the apostrophe in the sentence.

4. Dom can't find his pencil.
5. I'll hang up her coat.
6. They're walking to school.

School 26

Skill Sharpeners: Grammar and Punctuation • EMC 9951 • © Evan-Moor Corp.

Page 27

Punctuation Fun

Contractions Need Apostrophes!

Draw lines to connect two words to the matching contraction. Then write an apostrophe in the contraction. The first one is done for you.

should + not — shouldn't
did + not — didn't
you + will — you'll
do + not — don't

School 27

© Evan-Moor Corp. • EMC 9951 • Skill Sharpeners: Grammar and Punctuation

Page 28

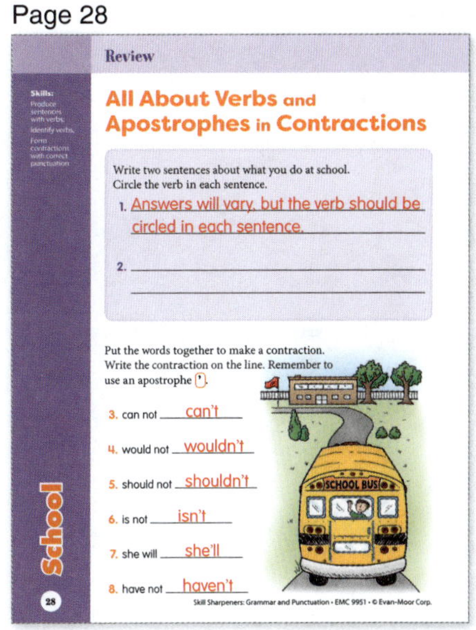
Review

All About Verbs and Apostrophes in Contractions

Write two sentences about what you do at school. Circle the verb in each sentence.

1. Answers will vary, but the verb should be circled in each sentence.
2.

Put the words together to make a contraction. Write the contraction on the line. Remember to use an apostrophe (').

3. can not can't
4. would not wouldn't
5. should not shouldn't
6. is not isn't
7. she will she'll
8. have not haven't

School 28

Skill Sharpeners: Grammar and Punctuation • EMC 9951 • © Evan-Moor Corp.

Page 29

Story

Read the story.

A Birthday Party

Today is Ryan's birthday party. Ryan invited all his friends to the party. **He** told **me** that the party starts at 3:00. **It** is 1:00 now. There will be pizza, cake, and balloons at the party. **I** will see Danielle. **She** is also Ryan's friend. I will bring Ryan a birthday gift. I hope he will like it. At 2:00, Mom and I wrap the gift together. **We** will put a ribbon on it. I can't wait for the party!

Read the rules. Answer the questions.

Grammar: A **pronoun** is a word that can take the place of a noun in a sentence.
How many blue **pronouns** can you find in the story? 6

Punctuation: When we write the time, we use a **colon** (:) between the hour and the minutes.
How many **colons** can you find in the story? 3

Find It!

Birthday Party 29

© Evan-Moor Corp. • EMC 9951 • Skill Sharpeners: Grammar and Punctuation

Page 30

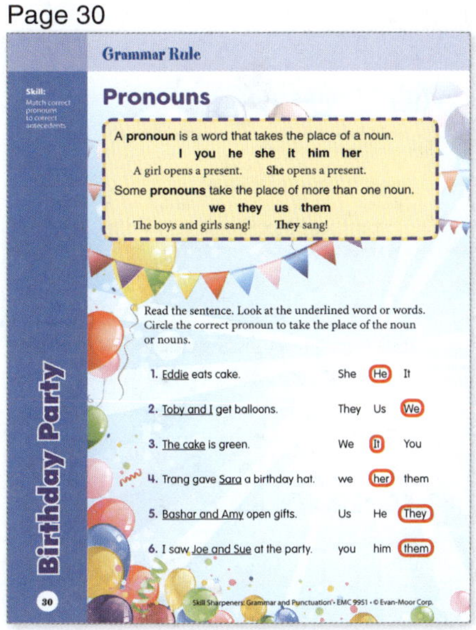
Grammar Rule

Pronouns

A **pronoun** is a word that takes the place of a noun.
I you he she it him her
A girl opens a present. **She** opens a present.
Some **pronouns** take the place of more than one noun.
we they us them
The boys and girls sang! **They** sang!

Read the sentence. Look at the underlined word or words. Circle the correct pronoun to take the place of the noun or nouns.

1. Eddie eats cake. She (He) It
2. Toby and I get balloons. They Us (We)
3. The cake is green. We (It) You
4. Trang gave Sara a birthday hat. we (her) them
5. Bashar and Amy open gifts. Us He (They)
6. I saw Joe and Sue at the party. you him (them)

Birthday Party 30

Skill Sharpeners: Grammar and Punctuation • EMC 9951 • © Evan-Moor Corp.

Page 31

Grammar Practice

The Perfect Pronoun

Look at the underlined word or words in the sentence. Write a pronoun to take the place of the common or proper noun.

I You He She It We They

1. Zoey and Jaya dance along with the music. They dance along with the music.
2. Pablo and I play a game at the party. We play a game at the party.
3. The girl invited her friends. She invited her friends.

Write a sentence with the pronoun **he**.

4. Answers will vary.

Birthday Party 31

© Evan-Moor Corp. • EMC 9951 • Skill Sharpeners: Grammar and Punctuation

To download a larger version of this answer key, go to: ***www.evan-moor.com/resources***
Enter your email address and this resource code: **EMC9951**

Page 32

Punctuation Rule

Colons in Time

When you write the time, use a **colon** (:) between the numbers that show the hour and the minutes.
The birthday party begins at 3:00.
We will cut the cake at 4:00.
The party ends at 5:00.

Read the sentence.
Write the colon in the time.

1. Jake leaves for the party at 2:00.
2. Mia leaves for the party at 2:30.
3. Timmy gets to John's house at 3:00.
4. John blows out the candles at 4:40.
5. John opens gifts at 5:15.
6. The children play games at 5:30.
7. All of John's friends leave at 6:20.
8. John goes to bed at 8:10.

Birthday Party

32

Page 33

Grammar Fun

Pronoun Match

Read the sentences. Fill in the circle next to the sentence that matches the picture.

1. ○ She grabs balloons. ● They grab balloons.
2. ● He blows out the candles. ○ We blow out the candles.
3. ● She makes a birthday wish. ○ He makes a birthday wish.
4. ○ The clown juggles us in the air. ● The clown juggles them in the air.

Birthday Party

33

Page 34

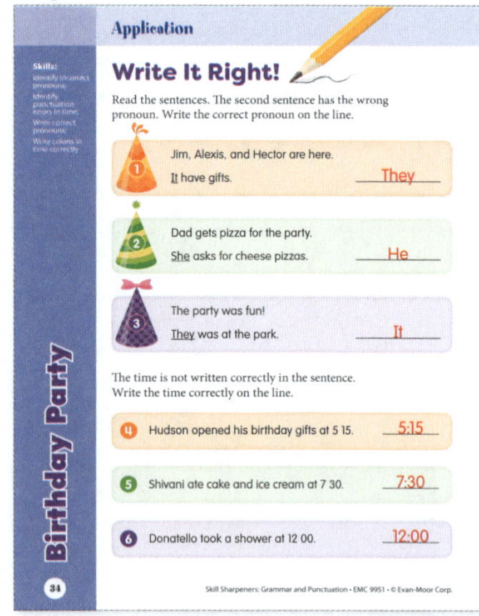

Application

Write It Right!

Read the sentences. The second sentence has the wrong pronoun. Write the correct pronoun on the line.

1. Jim, Alexis, and Hector are here. It have gifts. They
2. Dad gets pizza for the party. She asks for cheese pizzas. He
3. The party was fun! They was at the park. It

The time is not written correctly in the sentence. Write the time correctly on the line.

4. Hudson opened his birthday gifts at 5 15. 5:15
5. Shivani ate cake and ice cream at 7 30. 7:30
6. Donatello took a shower at 12 00. 12:00

Birthday Party

34

Page 35

Punctuation Fun

Fix the Watch

Terrell got a new watch as a birthday gift, but something is wrong with it. Write (:)s to fix the way it shows the time.

1. morning 8:00
2. lunch 12:30
3. dinner 5:45
4. bedtime 7:15

Birthday Party

35

Page 36

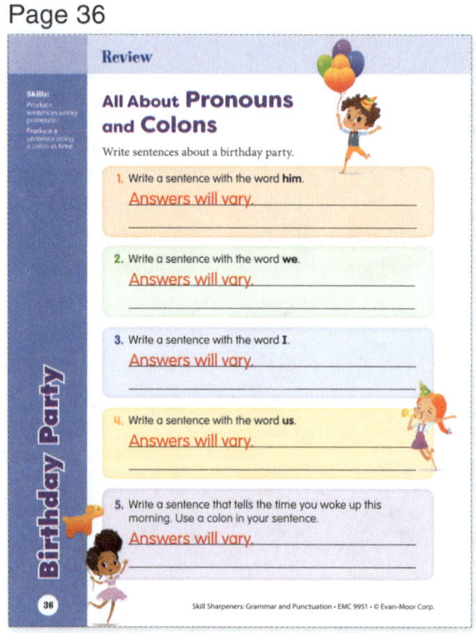

Review

All About Pronouns and Colons

Write sentences about a birthday party.

1. Write a sentence with the word **him**. Answers will vary.
2. Write a sentence with the word **we**. Answers will vary.
3. Write a sentence with the word **I**. Answers will vary.
4. Write a sentence with the word **us**. Answers will vary.
5. Write a sentence that tells the time you woke up this morning. Use a colon in your sentence. Answers will vary.

Birthday Party

36

Page 37

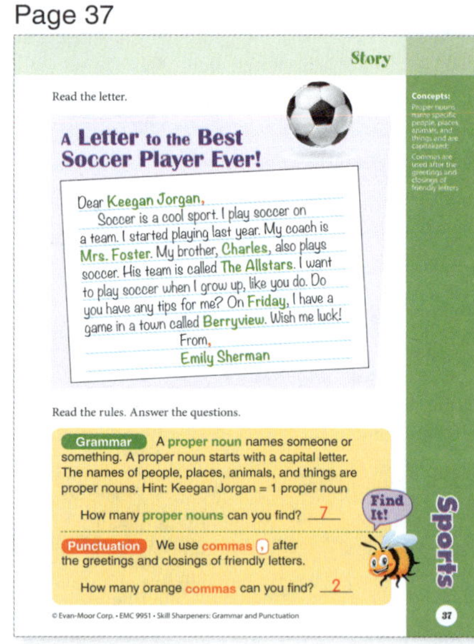

Story

Read the letter.

A Letter to the Best Soccer Player Ever!

Dear Keegan Jorgan,
Soccer is a cool sport. I play soccer on a team. I started playing last year. My coach is Mrs. Foster. My brother, Charles, also plays soccer. His team is called The Allstars. I want to play soccer when I grow up, like you do. Do you have any tips for me? On Friday, I have a game in a town called Berryview. Wish me luck!
From,
Emily Sherman

Read the rules. Answer the questions.

Grammar A proper noun names someone or something. A proper noun starts with a capital letter. The names of people, places, animals, and things are proper nouns. Hint: Keegan Jorgan = 1 proper noun

How many proper nouns can you find? 7

Punctuation We use commas (,) after the greetings and closings of friendly letters.

How many orange commas can you find? 2

Find It!

Sports

37

Page 38

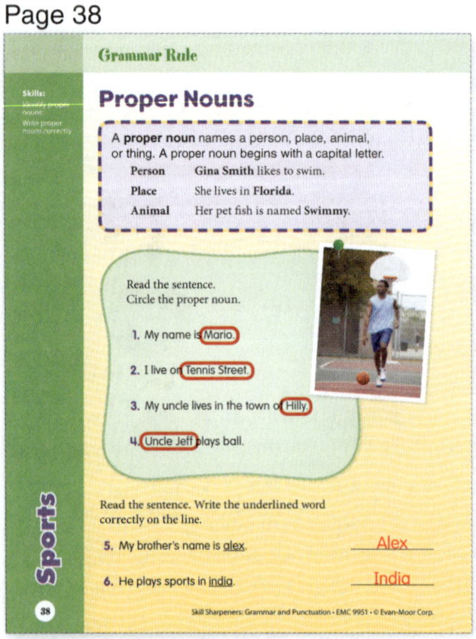

Grammar Rule

Proper Nouns

A **proper noun** names a person, place, animal, or thing. A proper noun begins with a capital letter.

Person	**Gina Smith** likes to swim.
Place	She lives in **Florida**.
Animal	Her pet fish is named **Swimmy**.

Read the sentence.
Circle the proper noun.

1. My name is (Mario).
2. I live on (Tennis Street).
3. My uncle lives in the town of (Hilly).
4. (Uncle Jeff) plays ball.

Read the sentence. Write the underlined word correctly on the line.

5. My brother's name is alex. Alex
6. He plays sports in india. India

Sports

38

Page 39

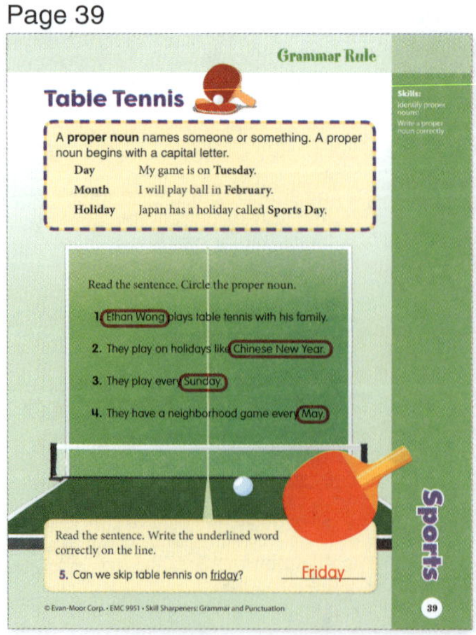

Grammar Rule

Table Tennis

A **proper noun** names someone or something. A proper noun begins with a capital letter.

Day	My game is on **Tuesday**.
Month	I will play ball in **February**.
Holiday	Japan has a holiday called **Sports Day**.

Read the sentence. Circle the proper noun.

1. (Ethan Wong) plays table tennis with his family.
2. They play on holidays like (Chinese New Year).
3. They play every (Sunday).
4. They have a neighborhood game every (May).

Read the sentence. Write the underlined word correctly on the line.

5. Can we skip table tennis on friday? Friday

Sports

39

Page 40

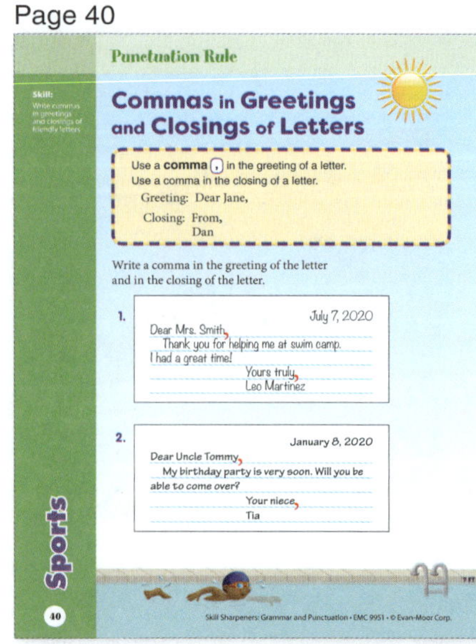

Punctuation Rule

Commas in Greetings and Closings of Letters

Use a **comma** (,) in the greeting of a letter.
Use a comma in the closing of a letter.
Greeting: Dear Jane,
Closing: From,
Dan

Write a comma in the greeting of the letter and in the closing of the letter.

1.
July 7, 2020
Dear Mrs. Smith,
Thank you for helping me at swim camp. I had a great time!
Yours truly,
Leo Martinez

2.
January 8, 2020
Dear Uncle Tommy,
My birthday party is very soon. Will you be able to come over?
Your niece,
Tia

Sports

40

To download a larger version of this answer key, go to: ***www.evan-moor.com/resources***
Enter your email address and this resource code: **EMC9951**

Page 41

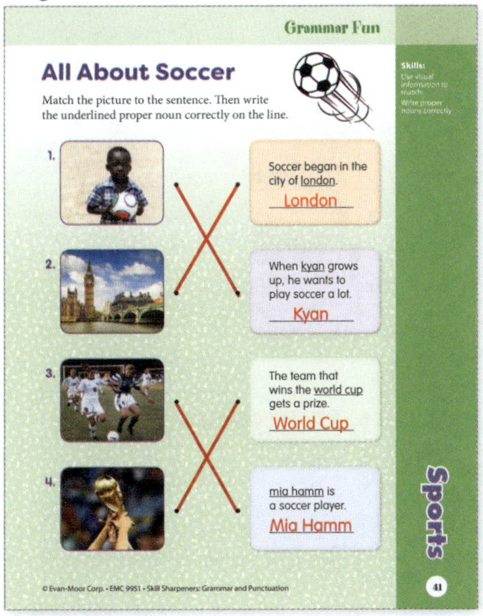
Grammar Fun

All About Soccer

Match the picture to the sentence. Then write the underlined proper noun correctly on the line.

1. Soccer began in the city of london. — London
2. When kyan grows up, he wants to play soccer a lot. — Kyan
3. The team that wins the world cup gets a prize. — World Cup
4. mia hamm is a soccer player. — Mia Hamm

Sports

Page 42

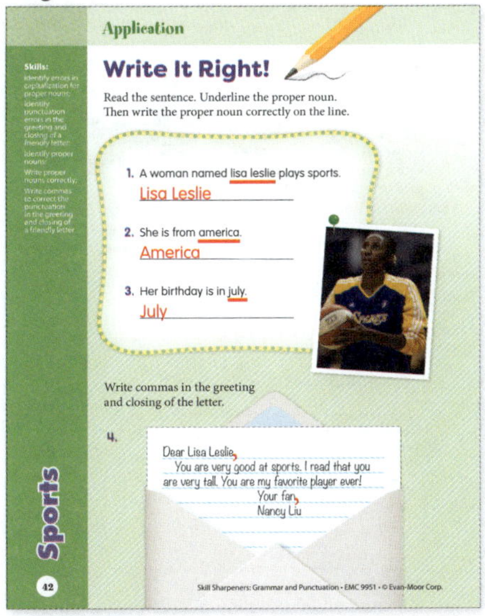
Application

Write It Right!

Read the sentence. Underline the proper noun. Then write the proper noun correctly on the line.

1. A woman named lisa leslie plays sports. — Lisa Leslie
2. She is from america. — America
3. Her birthday is in july. — July

Write commas in the greeting and closing of the letter.

4. Dear Lisa Leslie,
You are very good at sports. I read that you are very tall. You are my favorite player ever!
Your fan,
Nancy Liu

Sports

Page 43

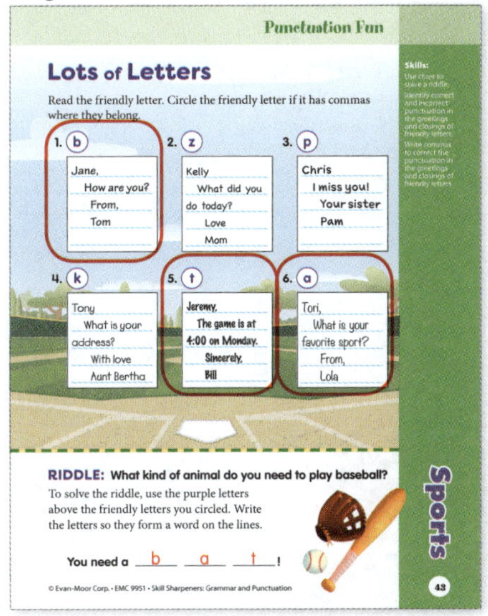
Punctuation Fun

Lots of Letters

Read the friendly letter. Circle the friendly letter if it has commas where they belong.

1. (b) Jane, How are you? From, Tom
2. (z) Kelly What did you do today? Love Mom
3. (p) Chris I miss you! Your sister Pam
4. (k) Tony What is your address? With love Aunt Bertha
5. (t) Jeremy, The game is at 4:00 on Monday. Sincerely, Bill
6. (a) Tori, What is your favorite sport? From, Lola

RIDDLE: What kind of animal do you need to play baseball?

To solve the riddle, use the purple letters above the friendly letters you circled. Write the letters so they form a word on the lines.

You need a b a t!

Sports

Page 44

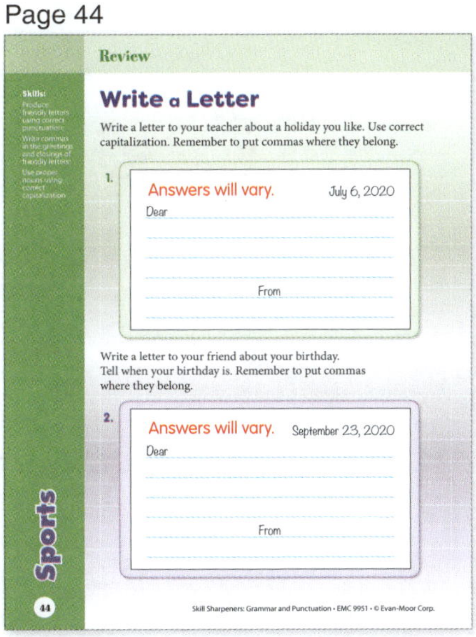
Review

Write a Letter

Write a letter to your teacher about a holiday you like. Use correct capitalization. Remember to put commas where they belong.

1. Answers will vary. July 6, 2020
Dear
From

Write a letter to your friend about your birthday. Tell when your birthday is. Remember to put commas where they belong.

2. Answers will vary. September 23, 2020
Dear
From

Sports

Page 45

Story

Read the story.

Planes, Planes, Planes

Have you ever been on a plane? I have! My first time was on Wednesday, January 10, 2018. It was so much fun! I could see the clouds. The people on the ground looked like little dots. I will fly to Disney World on March 4, 2019. We will drive our car to the airport. Then, off we will go! I will get lots of snacks to eat on the plane.

Read the rules. Answer the questions.

Grammar Some nouns name one person or thing. Some nouns name more than one.

How many blue nouns in the story name one? 3

How many green nouns name more than one? 4

Punctuation We use commas in dates between the day and the year.

How many orange commas in dates can you find? 2

Find It!

On the Move

Page 46

Grammar Rule

Singular and Plural Nouns

A noun can name one or more than one.
Add s to some nouns to name more than one.
Louis has one truck. Lila has two trucks.
Nate has one boat. Lovey has two boats.

Does the noun name one or more than one? Circle the correct picture.

1. trucks
2. train
3. cars
4. boat

On the Move

Page 47

Grammar Rule

Singular or Plural?

A noun can name one or more than one.
Singular nouns name one person or thing.
Plural nouns name more than one.
Add es to some nouns to name more than one.
Benito uses a brush.
The children use brushes.

Nadia rides the bus with her dad. She sees many things as she looks out the window. Circle the noun that goes with the picture.

1. box (boxes)
2. (bench) benches
3. bus (buses)
4. bush (bushes)

On the Move

Page 48

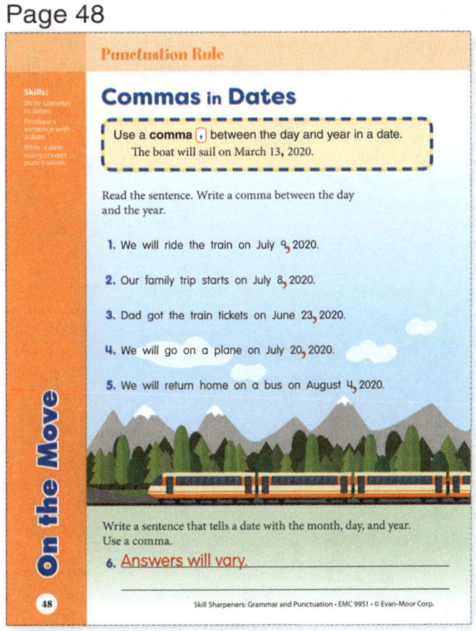
Punctuation Rule

Commas in Dates

Use a comma (,) between the day and year in a date.
The boat will sail on March 13, 2020.

Read the sentence. Write a comma between the day and the year.

1. We will ride the train on July 9, 2020.
2. Our family trip starts on July 8, 2020.
3. Dad got the train tickets on June 23, 2020.
4. We will go on a plane on July 20, 2020.
5. We will return home on a bus on August 4, 2020.

Write a sentence that tells a date with the month, day, and year. Use a comma.

6. Answers will vary.

On the Move

Page 49

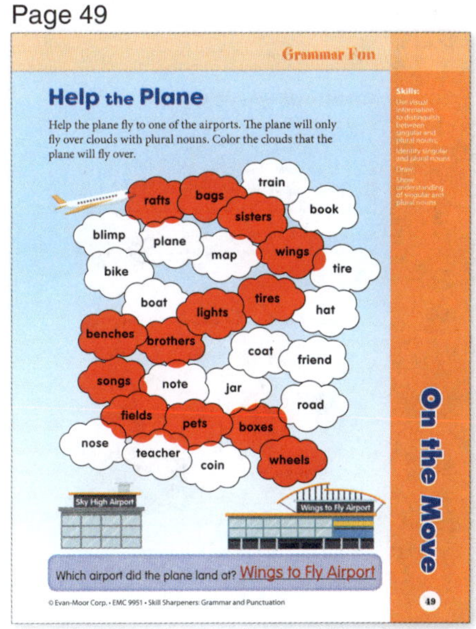
Grammar Fun

Help the Plane

Help the plane fly to one of the airports. The plane will only fly over clouds with plural nouns. Color the clouds that the plane will fly over.

rafts, bags, train, book, sisters, blimp, plane, map, wings, bike, tire, boat, lights, tires, hat, benches, brothers, coat, friend, songs, note, jar, road, fields, pets, boxes, nose, teacher, coin, wheels

Sky High Airport — Wings to Fly Airport

Which airport did the plane land at? Wings to Fly Airport

On the Move

To download a larger version of this answer key, go to: ***www.evan-moor.com/resources***
Enter your email address and this resource code: **EMC9951**

Page 50

Application

Write It Right!

Read the sentence. Write a comma if it is needed. Then write **one** or **more than one** to tell about the underlined noun.

1. I got a new wagon on April 7, 2017. — one
2. I see two rafts on the lake. — more than one
3. We'll get bikes on June 8, 2020. — more than one
4. The boat was on the river on July 2, 2017. — one
5. Can we get a new car? — one

On the Move — 50

Skill Sharpeners: Grammar and Punctuation • EMC 9951 • © Evan-Moor Corp.

Page 51

Punctuation Fun

What Carl Did

Read the story.

Carl rode on a bus on Friday. Friday was March 2, 2019. He rode a bike the next day, on Saturday. He rode on a boat on Sunday.

March						
Sun	Mon	Tues	Wed	Thur	Fri	Sat
					1	2	3
4	5	6	7	8	9	10
11	12	13	14	15	16	17
18	19	20	21	22	23	24
25	26	27	28	29	30	31

Write the date to finish the sentence. Then draw a picture of what Carl did that day.

1. The date on Saturday was March 3, 2019.

Drawing of a boy on a bike.

2. The date on Sunday was March 4, 2019.

Drawing of a boy on a boat.

© Evan-Moor Corp. • EMC 9951 • Skill Sharpeners: Grammar and Punctuation

On the Move — 51

Page 52

Review

On the Road, in the Sky

Look at the picture. Write the correct noun to finish the sentence.

1. There are 3 cars on the road. (car, cars)
2. There is a train on the tracks. (train, trains)
3. The plane is up in the sky. (plane, planes)

Read Robert's calendar. Write the date to answer the question. Remember to use a comma where it is needed.

Robert	October 2019					
Sunday	Monday	Tuesday	Wednesday	Thursday	Friday	Saturday
	1	2 Pick apples	3	4 John's birthday	5 Go fishing	6	7 Ride the ferry

4. On what date did Robert go fishing? October 5, 2019
5. What date did Robert ride the ferry? October 7, 2019

On the Move — 52

Skill Sharpeners: Grammar and Punctuation • EMC 9951 • © Evan-Moor Corp.

Page 53

Story

Read the story.

Family and Food

I have a big family. We love food. Dave loves to eat fruit. He eats apples, bananas, and oranges every day. Mom and Dad eat lots of carrots, beans, and peas. Grandma likes sweets. My cousins like eggs. We shop at the store. That's where my big sisters get gum, juice, and bread. Grandpa gets berries, milk, and crackers. There are so many good foods to eat!

Read the rules. Answer the questions.

Grammar A singular verb tells what one person does. A plural verb tells what more than one person does.

How many purple singular verbs can you find in the story? 4

How many green plural verbs can you find in the story? 5

Find It!

Punctuation Write a comma between each word in a list.

How many commas with words in a list can you find in the story? 8

© Evan-Moor Corp. • EMC 9951 • Skill Sharpeners: Grammar and Punctuation

Food — 53

Page 54

Grammar Rule

Verbs

A **verb** tells what one person or thing does. A verb can also tell what more than one person or thing does.

One: Jay **eats.** The dog **eats.**

More than one: Jay and Tom **eat.** The dogs **eat.**

Look at the picture. Write the correct verb on the line to finish the sentence.

1. Mom chops food for dinner. (chops, chop)
2. Kyle and Dad play with their food. (plays, play)
3. Mom and Dad hear a story at dinner. (hears, hear)
4. The baby loves eating. (loves, love)

Food — 54

Skill Sharpeners: Grammar and Punctuation • EMC 9951 • © Evan-Moor Corp.

Page 55

Grammar Practice

What Do You Eat at School?

Read the sentence. Write the correct verb on the line.

1. Tanya brings lunch in a brown bag. (brings, bring)
2. Ray and Denzel sit by the door at lunch. (sits, sit)
3. Mom makes a yummy lunch for Kenny. (makes, make)
4. Prisha and Jamie munch on crackers. (munches, munch)
5. Mrs. Wong helps Mario open his milk. (helps, help)

Write a sentence with a verb that tells about more than one.

6. Answers will vary.

© Evan-Moor Corp. • EMC 9951 • Skill Sharpeners: Grammar and Punctuation

Food — 55

Page 56

Punctuation Rule

Commas with Words in a List

Use a **comma** between words in a list. Write a comma before the word **and**.

My sister bakes cookies, cakes, and pies.

She uses milk, butter, salt, and sugar.

Read the sentence. It is missing commas. Write a comma between each word in a list.

1. I pack lunch on Monday, Tuesday, and Friday.
2. Every day I eat toast, fruit, cheese, and yogurt.
3. Janet washes her spoon, fork, and plate.

Look at the picture. Write a sentence that tells three things you see. Write a comma between each thing.

4. Answers will vary.

Food — 56

Skill Sharpeners: Grammar and Punctuation • EMC 9951 • © Evan-Moor Corp.

Page 57

Grammar Fun

Food, Food, Food

Read the sentence. Write the correct verb. Then draw a line to match the picture to the sentence.

1. They eat dinner. (eat, eats)
2. They shop together. (shop, shops)
3. Dante stirs the cake batter. (stir, stirs)
4. She looks at the food on the plate. (look, looks)

© Evan-Moor Corp. • EMC 9951 • Skill Sharpeners: Grammar and Punctuation

Food — 57

Page 58

Application

Write It Right!

The sentence has the wrong verb. Write the correct verb on the line.

1. Jan shop for food. — shops
2. The hot dogs looks yummy. — look
3. Kim and Yun makes dinner. — make

Write the missing commas in the sentence.

4. I eat an egg, toast, and a banana in the morning.
5. My family has juice, pasta, salad, and bread at dinner.

Food — 58

Skill Sharpeners: Grammar and Punctuation • EMC 9951 • © Evan-Moor Corp.

To download a larger version of this answer key, go to: ***www.evan-moor.com/resources***
Enter your email address and this resource code: **EMC9951**

Page 59

Punctuation Fun

Three Foods

Look at the pictures. Follow the directions.

fork spoon bowl plate

1. Write a sentence that lists three things in the pictures that you have at your house. Use commas.
Answers will vary.

sandwich milk carrot sticks crackers

2. Write a sentence that lists three foods in the pictures that you would eat for lunch. Use commas.
Answers will vary.

cake ice cream cone berries pie

3. Write a sentence that lists three foods in the pictures that you would eat for dessert. Use commas.
Answers will vary.

Skills: Produce sentences with series using correct punctuation. Use visual information to produce sentences. Use commas to separate items in a series.

Food

59

Page 60

Review

All About Food

Read the sentence. Is the verb correct? Circle **yes** or **no**.

1. Dale needs bread and milk. (yes) no
2. Mickey eat a lot. yes (no)
3. Lindsey writes a book about food. (yes) no

Read the sentence. Are there commas in the right place? Circle **yes** or **no**.

4. Burt wants peas carrots and rice. yes (no)
5. Blake finds a spoon, bowl, fork, and plate. (yes) no

Skills: Identify correct and incorrect use of subject-verb agreement. Identify correct and incorrect use of commas to separate items in a series.

Food

60

Page 61

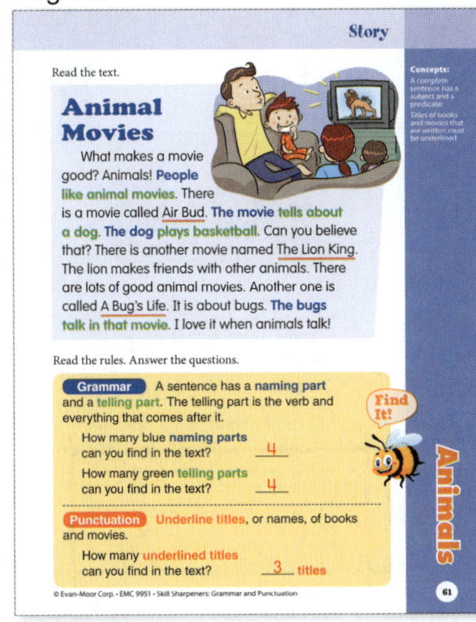

Story

Read the text.

Animal Movies

What makes a movie good? Animals! **People like animal movies.** There is a movie called Air Bud. **The movie tells about a dog. The dog plays basketball.** Can you believe that? There is another movie named The Lion King. The lion makes friends with other animals. There are lots of good animal movies. Another one is called A Bug's Life. It is about bugs. **The bugs talk in that movie.** I love it when animals talk!

Read the rules. Answer the questions.

Grammar A sentence has a **naming part** and a **telling part**. The telling part is the verb and everything that comes after it.

How many blue **naming parts** can you find in the text? 4

How many green **telling parts** can you find in the text? 4

Find It!

Punctuation Underline titles, or names, of books and movies.

How many underlined titles can you find in the text? 3 titles

Concepts: A complete sentence has a subject and a predicate. Titles of books and movies that are written must be underlined.

Animals

61

Page 62

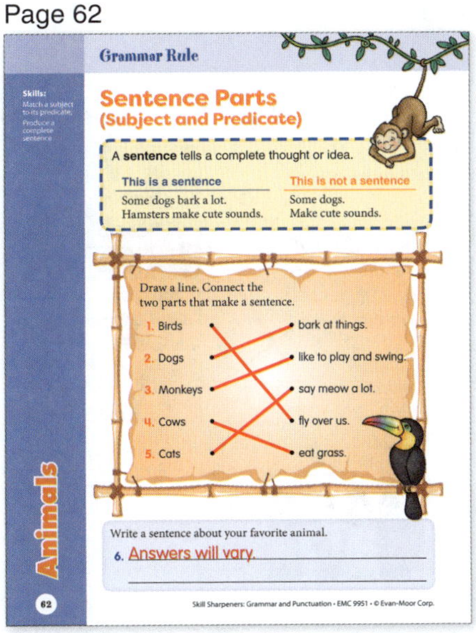

Grammar Rule

Sentence Parts (Subject and Predicate)

A **sentence** tells a complete thought or idea.

This is a sentence	This is not a sentence
Some dogs bark a lot. Hamsters make cute sounds.	Some dogs. Make cute sounds.

Draw a line. Connect the two parts that make a sentence.

1. Birds — bark at things.
2. Dogs — like to play and swing.
3. Monkeys — say meow a lot.
4. Cows — fly over us.
5. Cats — eat grass.

Write a sentence about your favorite animal.

6. Answers will vary.

Skills: Match a subject to its predicate. Produce a complete sentence.

Animals

62

Page 63

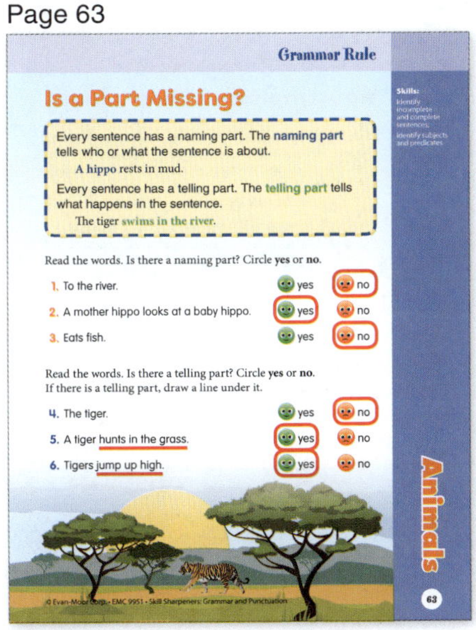

Grammar Rule

Is a Part Missing?

Every sentence has a naming part. The **naming part** tells who or what the sentence is about.

A **hippo** rests in mud.

Every sentence has a telling part. The **telling part** tells what happens in the sentence.

The tiger **swims in the river.**

Read the words. Is there a naming part? Circle **yes** or **no**.

1. To the river. yes (no)
2. A mother hippo looks at a baby hippo. (yes) no
3. Eats fish. yes (no)

Read the words. Is there a telling part? Circle **yes** or **no**. If there is a telling part, draw a line under it.

4. The tiger. yes (no)
5. A tiger <u>hunts in the grass</u>. (yes) no
6. Tigers <u>jump up high</u>. (yes) no

Skills: Identify incomplete and complete sentences. Identify subjects and predicates.

Animals

63

Page 64

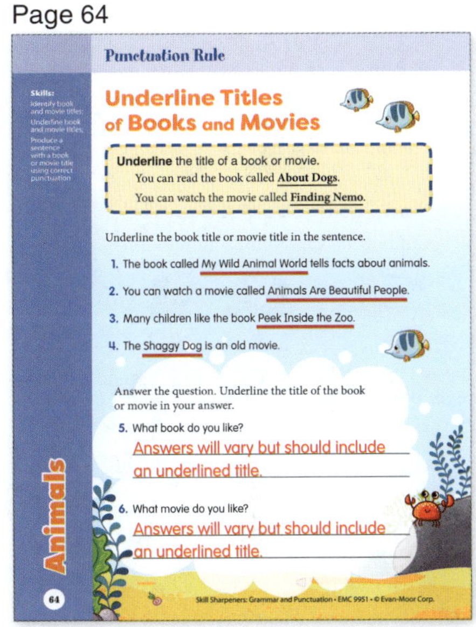

Punctuation Rule

Underline Titles of Books and Movies

Underline the title of a book or movie.

You can read the book called <u>About Dogs</u>.

You can watch the movie called <u>Finding Nemo</u>.

Underline the book title or movie title in the sentence.

1. The book called <u>My Wild Animal World</u> tells facts about animals.
2. You can watch a movie called <u>Animals Are Beautiful People</u>.
3. Many children like the book <u>Peek Inside the Zoo</u>.
4. The <u>Shaggy Dog</u> is an old movie.

Answer the question. Underline the title of the book or movie in your answer.

5. What book do you like?
Answers will vary but should include an underlined title.

6. What movie do you like?
Answers will vary but should include an underlined title.

Skills: Identify book and movie titles. Underline book and movie titles. Produce a sentence with a book or movie title using correct punctuation.

Animals

64

Page 65

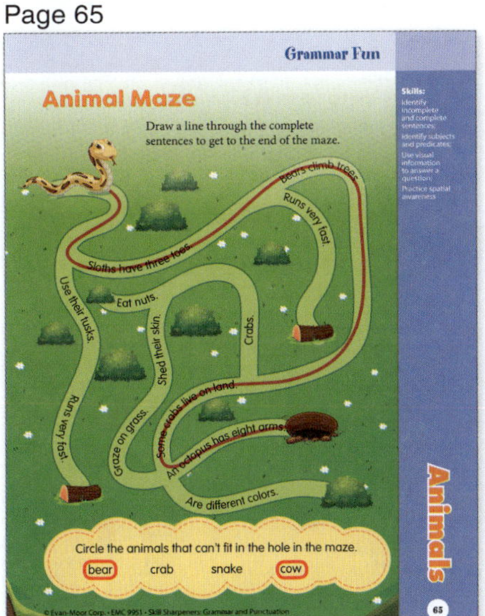

Grammar Fun

Animal Maze

Draw a line through the complete sentences to get to the end of the maze.

Circle the animals that can't fit in the hole in the maze.

(bear) crab snake (cow)

Skills: Identify incomplete and complete sentences. Identify subjects and predicates. Use visual information to answer a question. Practice spatial awareness.

Animals

65

Page 66

Application

Write It Right!

The sentences have a part missing. Circle **naming part** or **telling part** to show what is missing.

1. The whale. naming part (telling part)
2. Sits in the mud. (naming part) telling part
3. All the cows. naming part (telling part)

The sentence has a title that is written incorrectly. Write the title correctly on the line.

4. You can see the movie called The Secret Life of Pets.
<u>The Secret Life of Pets</u>

5. The book Dogs and Puppies has a lot of facts.
<u>Dogs and Puppies</u>

6. The movie Stuart Little is about a mouse.
<u>Stuart Little</u>

Skills: Identify subjects and predicates. Write the title of a book or movie using correct punctuation. Identify book and movie titles.

Animals

66

Page 67

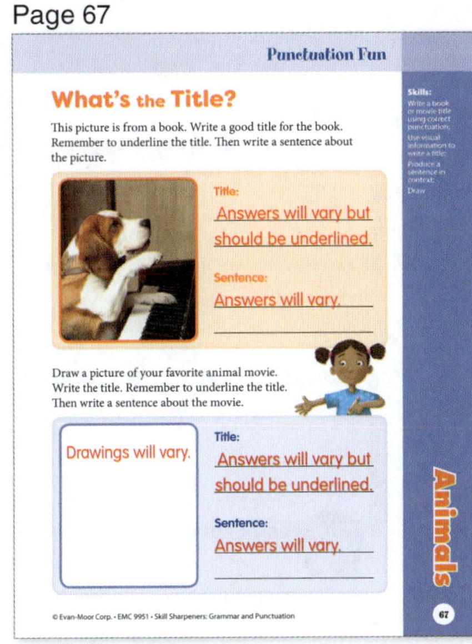

Punctuation Fun

What's the Title?

This picture is from a book. Write a good title for the book. Remember to underline the title. Then write a sentence about the picture.

Title: Answers will vary but should be underlined.

Sentence: Answers will vary.

Draw a picture of your favorite animal movie. Write the title. Remember to underline the title. Then write a sentence about the movie.

Drawings will vary.

Title: Answers will vary but should be underlined.

Sentence: Answers will vary.

Skills: Write a book or movie title using correct punctuation. Use visual information to write a title. Produce a sentence in context. Draw.

Animals

67

To download a larger version of this answer key, go to: ***www.evan-moor.com/resources***
Enter your email address and this resource code: **EMC9951**

Page 68

Review

At the Farm

Look at the picture. Then use a word group from the box to finish each sentence about the picture.

Word Box
The zebras
sprays the zebras with water
The water

1. The elephant sprays the zebras with water
2. The zebras get wet in the water.
3. The water makes a puddle on the ground.

Write one sentence about a book you like. Remember to underline the title.

4. Answers will vary but should be underlined.

Animals

Page 69

Story

Read the story.

Our Big Sale!

My family's yard sale is tomorrow! We have one every year. We sell a lot of stuff that we do not use anymore. Let me tell you what is for sale. My dad's fishing pole is five dollars. My mom's fish tank is six dollars. My sisters' bikes are ten dollars. My brother's toy car is two dollars. My two dogs' leashes are one dollar each. My parents' hats are four dollars each. I hope a lot of people come over to buy our stuff!

Read the rules. Answer the questions.

Grammar A singular possessive noun shows that something belongs to one person, animal, or thing. A plural possessive noun shows that something belongs to more than one person, animal, or thing.

How many singular possessive nouns can you find? 4

How many plural possessive nouns can you find? 3

Punctuation Possessive nouns always have an apostrophe (').

How many apostrophes can you find? 7

Family

Page 70

Grammar Rule

Possessive Nouns

A **possessive noun** shows that something belongs to a person, animal, or thing. It has an **apostrophe** (').

My **dad's** hat is red.
The hat belongs to my dad.

Circle the possessive noun in the sentence.

1. (Mom's) hair is brown.
2. (Rick's) arm is broken.
3. My sister is at (Dana's) house.
4. (Granny's) house smells like cookies.
5. My (dog's) tail is short.
6. Where is (John's) book?

Read the sentence. Then answer the question.

7. Mom's hair is long!
To whom does the hair belong? Mom

Family

Page 71

Grammar Rule

Plural Possessive Nouns

A **plural possessive noun** shows that something belongs to **more than one** person, animal, or thing. Many plural possessive nouns end with a (').

The **twins'** shirts are blue.
The shirts belong to the twins.

Read the words. Fill in the circle to tell about the picture.

1. the girls' shoes
2. The dogs' bowls
3. the cats' yarn
4. the boys' ball

Family

Page 72

Punctuation Rule

Apostrophes with Possessives

We put an **apostrophe** (') and an **s** at the end of most nouns to make them possessive. When a plural noun ends in **s**, we put only an **apostrophe** at the end to make it possessive.

Singular: The boy's coat is small.
Plural: The boys' coats are small.

Write (') or (') and **s** to show that something belongs to someone.

1. Where is Zayne's cup?
2. The beds' pillows are all clean.
3. The cats' toys are in the basket.
4. Have you seen Grandma's pen?
5. Aunt Elise made the girls' snack.

Family

Page 73

Grammar Fun

Match It!

Draw a line to match the words to the correct picture.

1. my brother's glasses
2. my sisters' book
3. my brothers' glasses
4. my sister's book

Look at the picture. Then circle the words that go with the picture.

5. childrens backpacks
(children's backpacks)

Family

Page 74

Application

Write It Right!

Read the sentence. Is the possessive noun correct? Circle **yes** or **no**.

1. My moms shoes are orange. yes (no)
2. Where are Vince's glasses? (yes) no
3. Our familys van is messy. yes (no)

The possessive noun in the sentence is not correct. Write it correctly on the line.

4. Papas pen is on the table. Papa's
5. We put up my four uncles pictures. uncles'

Family

Page 75

Punctuation Fun

Look at the Apostrophes

Look at the picture. Fill in the circle next to the words that tell about the picture.

1. ● Auntie Claire's hat ○ Auntie Claires hat
2. ○ the kitten's baskets ● the kittens' baskets
3. ● the cake's candles ○ the cakes' candles
4. ○ the flower's petals ● the flowers' petals

Family

Page 76

Review

Whose Is It?

Read the sentence. Write an apostrophe in the possessive noun.

1. Dad's mug has white dots.
2. Mom's mug looks like a rainbow.
3. Auntie Erin's mug has flowers.
4. My grandparents' mugs are yellow.
5. My two sisters' mugs are mostly pink.

Look at the family's mugs. The sentences above have clues to tell you who each mug belongs to. Write a possessive noun to tell whose mug it is.

6. Dad's mug
7. Auntie Erin's mug
8. Mom's mug
9. my two sisters' mugs

Family

To download a larger version of this answer key, go to: **www.evan-moor.com/resources**
Enter your email address and this resource code: **EMC9951**

Page 77

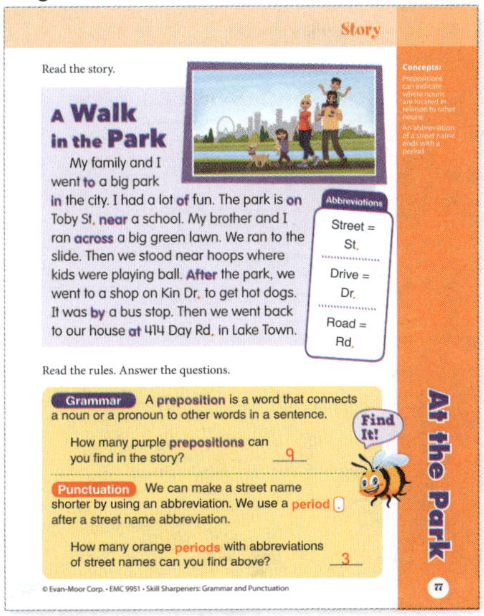
Story

Read the story.

A Walk in the Park

My family and I went to a big park in the city. I had a lot of fun. The park is on Toby St. near a school. My brother and I ran across a big green lawn. We ran to the slide. Then we stood near hoops where kids were playing ball. After the park, we went to a shop on Kin Dr. to get hot dogs. It was by a bus stop. Then we went back to our house at 414 Day Rd. in Lake Town.

Abbreviations: Street = St. Drive = Dr. Road = Rd.

Read the rules. Answer the questions.

Grammar: A **preposition** is a word that connects a noun or a pronoun to other words in a sentence.

How many purple **prepositions** can you find in the story? 9

Punctuation: We can make a street name shorter by using an abbreviation. We use a **period** after a street name abbreviation.

How many orange **periods** with abbreviations of street names can you find above? 3

At the Park 77

Page 78

Grammar Rule

Prepositions

Some words that tell **where** are called **prepositions**.
Melissa is **in** the pool.
Tom is **at** the park.
These words are prepositions:
on in under for to behind onto

Look at the pictures. Finish each sentence. Use a preposition from the box.

in on down over

1. The girl slides down the slide.
2. The children are in the sandbox.
3. The bird flies over the park.
4. The children play on the swings.

78 At the Park

Page 79

Grammar Practice

Prepositions in Sentences

Read the preposition. Read the sentence. Write the preposition to finish the sentence.

1. on — The children run on the grass.
2. into — Justin crawls into the tunnel.
3. under — Jenna reads a book under the tree.
4. between — Javier stands between the gates.
5. by — I will wait by the big tree.
6. over — The sun shines over the park.

At the Park 79

Page 80

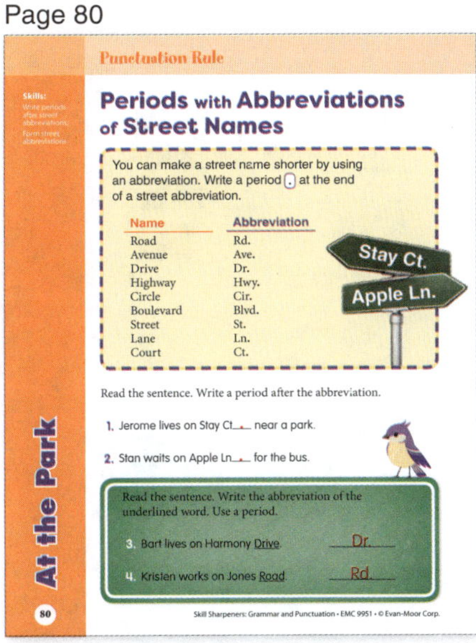
Punctuation Rule

Periods with Abbreviations of Street Names

You can make a street name shorter by using an abbreviation. Write a period at the end of a street abbreviation.

Name	Abbreviation
Road	Rd.
Avenue	Ave.
Drive	Dr.
Highway	Hwy.
Circle	Cir.
Boulevard	Blvd.
Street	St.
Lane	Ln.
Court	Ct.

Stay Ct. / Apple Ln.

Read the sentence. Write a period after the abbreviation.

1. Jerome lives on Stay Ct. near a park.
2. Stan waits on Apple Ln. for the bus.

Read the sentence. Write the abbreviation of the underlined word. Use a period.

3. Bart lives on Harmony Drive. Dr.
4. Kristen works on Jones Road. Rd.

80 At the Park

Page 81

Grammar Fun

All in the Picture

Look at the picture. Then answer the questions.

1. How many birds are **on** the trees? 6 birds
2. How many children are **near** the birds? 2 children

Look at the picture. Then answer the questions.

3. How many children are **on** the swings? 2 children
4. How many children go **down** the slide? 1 child or children

At the Park 81

Page 82

Application

Write It Right!

Does the sentence tell what the picture shows? Circle **yes** or **no**.

1. The picnic table is on the food. yes **no**
2. The tree sits under the girl. yes **no**
3. The boy sits in the tire swing. **yes** no

The abbreviation is missing a period. Fix the sentence.

4. Shell Blvd. is where Toni lives.
5. Take Lemon Ave. to get to the park.
6. The best park is on Leeds Rd. by the school.

82 At the Park

Page 83

Punctuation Fun

Street Signs

Look at the street signs. Answer the questions with abbreviations. Use periods.

Barking Lane / Yummy Drive / Apple Road / Puddle Street

1. Where do a lot of dogs live? Barking Ln.
2. Where do a lot of trees grow? Apple Rd.
3. Where does it rain a lot? Puddle St.
4. Where are there picnic tables? Yummy Dr.
5. The street signs need pictures. Draw a picture on each sign. Then color the signs and pictures. Drawings will vary.

At the Park 83

Page 84

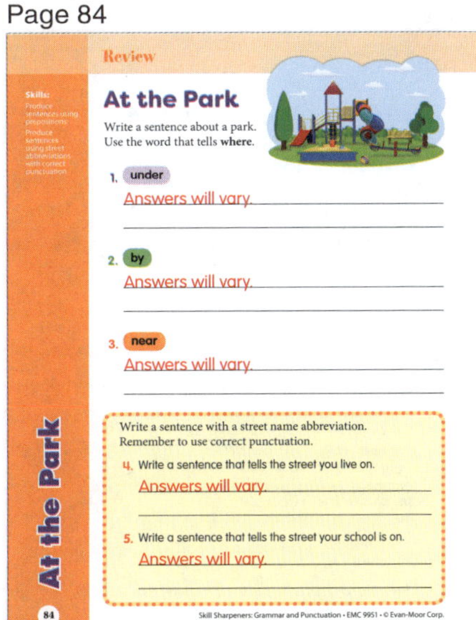
Review

At the Park

Write a sentence about a park. Use the word that tells **where**.

1. under — Answers will vary.
2. by — Answers will vary.
3. near — Answers will vary.

Write a sentence with a street name abbreviation. Remember to use correct punctuation.

4. Write a sentence that tells the street you live on. Answers will vary.
5. Write a sentence that tells the street your school is on. Answers will vary.

84 At the Park

Page 85

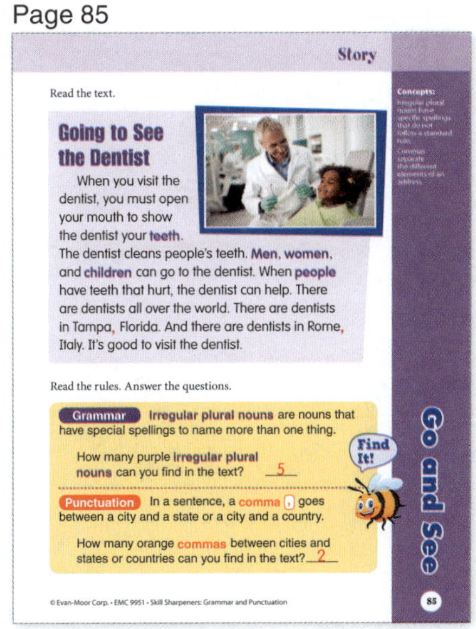
Story

Read the text.

Going to See the Dentist

When you visit the dentist, you must open your mouth to show the dentist your teeth. The dentist cleans people's teeth. Men, women, and children can go to the dentist. When people have teeth that hurt, the dentist can help. There are dentists all over the world. There are dentists in Tampa, Florida. And there are dentists in Rome, Italy. It's good to visit the dentist.

Read the rules. Answer the questions.

Grammar: **Irregular plural nouns** are nouns that have special spellings to name more than one thing.

How many purple **irregular plural nouns** can you find in the text? 5

Punctuation: In a sentence, a **comma** goes between a city and a state or a city and a country.

How many orange **commas** between cities and states or countries can you find in the text? 2

Go and See 85

To download a larger version of this answer key, go to: ***www.evan-moor.com/resources***
Enter your email address and this resource code: **EMC9951**

Page 86

Grammar Rule

Irregular Plural Nouns

Skills: Identify irregular plural nouns. Match irregular plural nouns to their singular forms.

Some nouns have special spellings to name **more than one**.

one mouse	two **mice**
one goose	two **geese**
one ox	two **oxen**
one wolf	two **wolves**

People like to see animals. Draw a line to match the word that names one to the word that names more than one.

1. goose — oxen
2. ox — wolves
3. mouse — geese
4. wolf — mice

Read the sentence. Circle the noun that has a special spelling to name more than one.

5. (Children) like to go to the zoo.
6. Can (people) feed an animal there?
7. The (geese) eat together.

Go and See 86

Skill Sharpeners: Grammar and Punctuation • EMC 9951 • © Evan-Moor Corp.

Page 87

Grammar Practice

Going to See the Lake

Skills: Write irregular plural nouns. Use irregular plural nouns. Use visual information. Distinguish between correct and incorrect forms of irregular plural nouns.

Read the special nouns in the box. Write the best noun to finish the sentence. HINT: Some nouns have the same spelling for one and more than one.

sheep deer geese fish

1. There are fish in the lake.
2. Young deer have spots on their fur.
3. Large geese fly over the lake.
4. Fluffy sheep say "baa" near the lake.

Circle the correct words that tell about the picture.

5. two wolf / (two wolves)
6. three fishies / (three fish)
7. (three sheep) / three sheeps

Go and See 87

© Evan-Moor Corp. • EMC 9951 • Skill Sharpeners: Grammar and Punctuation

Page 88

Punctuation Rule

Commas Between City and State or City and Country

Skill: Write commas to separate the city from the state or the city from the country in an address.

When you write an address, use a **comma** (,) between the city and the state.
350 Fifth Ave.
New York, NY 10118

In a sentence, use a comma between a city and state or a city and country.
There is an art museum in Dallas, Texas.
There is a lot to see in Beijing, China.

The sentence is missing a comma. Write the comma.

1. Disney World is in Orlando, Florida.
2. There is a beautiful tower in Seoul, South Korea.
3. You can take a plane to Cairo, Egypt.
4. You can visit President Abraham Lincoln's old house in Springfield, Illinois.

Go and See 88

Skill Sharpeners: Grammar and Punctuation • EMC 9951 • © Evan-Moor Corp.

Page 89

Grammar Fun

Going to the Market

Skills: Use visual information to show understanding of irregular plural nouns. Recognize irregular plural nouns.

Are the irregular plural nouns below shown in the picture? Circle **yes** or **no**. Then color the picture. HINT: Remember, **plural** means **more than one**. Circle **yes** if there is more than one.

women	(yes)	no	mice	(yes)	no
men	(yes)	no	children	(yes)	no
geese	yes	(no)	feet	(yes)	no

Go and See 89

© Evan-Moor Corp. • EMC 9951 • Skill Sharpeners: Grammar and Punctuation

Page 90

Application

Write It Right!

Skills: Form irregular plural nouns. Identify incorrect forms of irregular plural nouns. Write commas to separate cities from countries.

Read the sentence. The irregular plural noun is wrong. Write it correctly on the line.

1. Mouses can be brown or white. Mice
2. Sheeps have wool that keeps them warm. Sheep
3. Deers can be playful. Deer

The sentence is missing a comma. Write a comma to fix the sentence.

4. Lots of animals live near Halifax, Canada.
5. There is an animal park in Nairobi, Kenya.
6. You can see koalas in Brisbane, Australia.

Go and See 90

Skill Sharpeners: Grammar and Punctuation • EMC 9951 • © Evan-Moor Corp.

Page 91

Punctuation Fun

Let's Mail a Letter!

Skills: Write commas to separate cities from states in addresses. Write complete addresses with correct punctuation.

Write the commas on the envelope so it can be mailed.

1500 Cassie St.
Monterey, CA 93940

Fun Land
1211 Fun Land Dr.
Anaheim, CA 92802

Now write addresses on this envelope so it can be mailed. Remember to write commas.

Answers will vary.

Go and See 91

© Evan-Moor Corp. • EMC 9951 • Skill Sharpeners: Grammar and Punctuation

Page 92

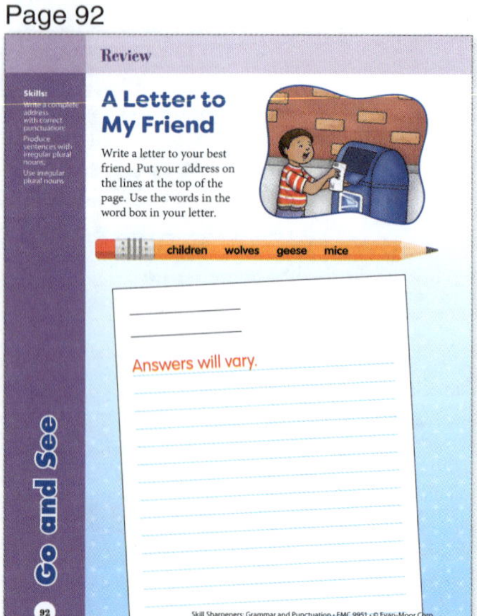
Review

A Letter to My Friend

Skills: Write a complete address with correct punctuation. Produce sentences with irregular plural nouns. Use irregular plural nouns.

Write a letter to your best friend. Put your address on the lines at the top of the page. Use the words in the word box in your letter.

children wolves geese mice

Answers will vary.

Go and See 92

Skill Sharpeners: Grammar and Punctuation • EMC 9951 • © Evan-Moor Corp.

Page 93

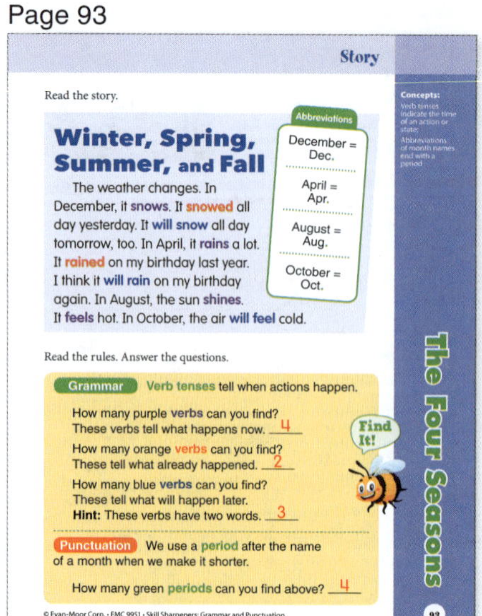
Story

Concepts: Verb tenses indicate the time of an action or state. Abbreviations of month names end with a period.

Read the story.

Winter, Spring, Summer, and Fall

The weather changes. In December, it **snows**. It **snowed** all day yesterday. It **will snow** all day tomorrow, too. In April, it **rains** a lot. It **rained** on my birthday last year. I think it **will rain** on my birthday again. In August, the sun **shines**. It **feels** hot. In October, the air **will feel** cold.

Abbreviations
December = Dec.
April = Apr.
August = Aug.
October = Oct.

Read the rules. Answer the questions.

Grammar Verb tenses tell when actions happen.

How many purple verbs can you find? These verbs tell what happens now. 4
How many orange verbs can you find? These tell what already happened. 2
How many blue verbs can you find? These tell what will happen later. **Hint:** These verbs have two words. 3

Find It!

Punctuation We use a **period** after the name of a month when we make it shorter.

How many green periods can you find above? 4

The Four Seasons 93

© Evan-Moor Corp. • EMC 9951 • Skill Sharpeners: Grammar and Punctuation

Page 94

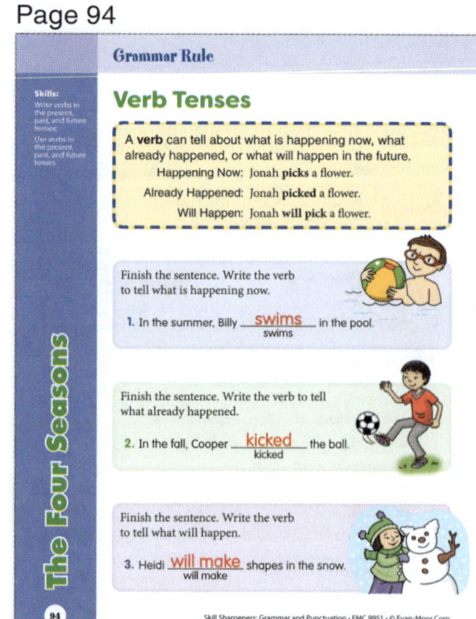
Grammar Rule

Verb Tenses

Skills: Write verbs in the present, past, and future tenses. Use verbs in the present, past, and future tenses.

A **verb** can tell about what is happening now, what already happened, or what will happen in the future.
Happening Now: Jonah **picks** a flower.
Already Happened: Jonah **picked** a flower.
Will Happen: Jonah **will pick** a flower.

Finish the sentence. Write the verb to tell what is happening now.

1. In the summer, Billy swims in the pool. (swims)

Finish the sentence. Write the verb to tell what already happened.

2. In the fall, Cooper kicked the ball. (kicked)

Finish the sentence. Write the verb to tell what will happen.

3. Heidi will make shapes in the snow. (will make)

The Four Seasons 94

Skill Sharpeners: Grammar and Punctuation • EMC 9951 • © Evan-Moor Corp.

To download a larger version of this answer key, go to: ***www.evan-moor.com/resources***
Enter your email address and this resource code: **EMC9951**

Page 95

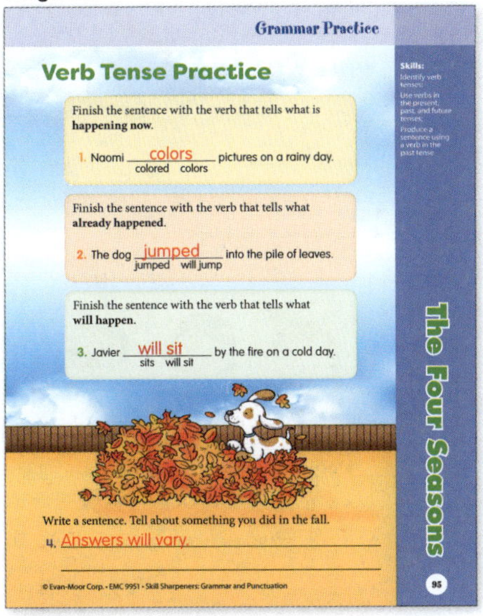
Grammar Practice

Verb Tense Practice

Finish the sentence with the verb that tells what is **happening now**.

1. Naomi __colors__ pictures on a rainy day. (colored / colors)

Finish the sentence with the verb that tells what **already happened**.

2. The dog __jumped__ into the pile of leaves. (jumped / will jump)

Finish the sentence with the verb that tells what **will happen**.

3. Javier __will sit__ by the fire on a cold day. (sits / will sit)

Write a sentence. Tell about something you did in the fall.

4. Answers will vary.

The Four Seasons

© Evan-Moor Corp. • EMC 9951 • Skill Sharpeners: Grammar and Punctuation — 95

Page 96

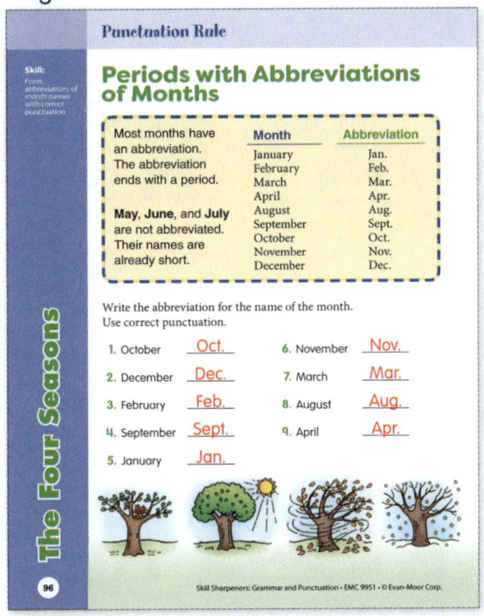
Punctuation Rule

Periods with Abbreviations of Months

Most months have an abbreviation. The abbreviation ends with a period.

May, **June**, and **July** are not abbreviated. Their names are already short.

Month	Abbreviation
January	Jan.
February	Feb.
March	Mar.
April	Apr.
August	Aug.
September	Sept.
October	Oct.
November	Nov.
December	Dec.

Write the abbreviation for the name of the month. Use correct punctuation.

1. October __Oct.__
2. December __Dec.__
3. February __Feb.__
4. September __Sept.__
5. January __Jan.__
6. November __Nov.__
7. March __Mar.__
8. August __Aug.__
9. April __Apr.__

The Four Seasons

96 — Skill Sharpeners: Grammar and Punctuation • EMC 9951 • © Evan-Moor Corp.

Page 97

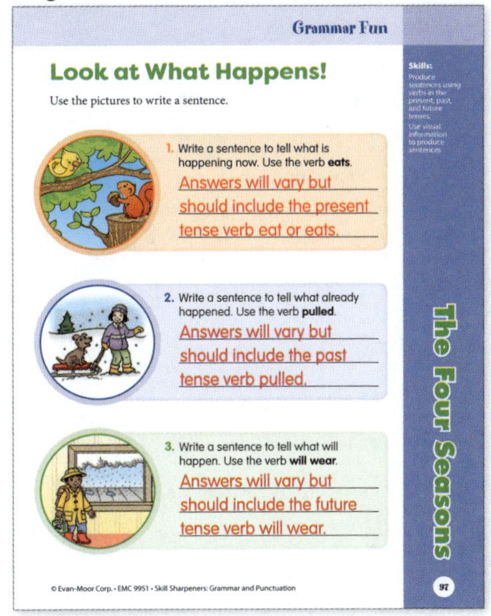
Grammar Fun

Look at What Happens!

Use the pictures to write a sentence.

1. Write a sentence to tell what is happening now. Use the verb **eats**.
Answers will vary but should include the present tense verb eat or eats.

2. Write a sentence to tell what already happened. Use the verb **pulled**.
Answers will vary but should include the past tense verb pulled.

3. Write a sentence to tell what will happen. Use the verb **will wear**.
Answers will vary but should include the future tense verb will wear.

The Four Seasons

© Evan-Moor Corp. • EMC 9951 • Skill Sharpeners: Grammar and Punctuation — 97

Page 98

Application

Write It Right!

Write the sentence so it tells what is **happening now**.

1. I will play in the snow.
I play in the snow.

Write the sentence so it tells what **already happened**.

2. I jump in the puddle.
I jumped in the puddle.

Write the sentence so it tells what **will happen**.

3. I ride the bike.
I will ride the bike.

Read the sentence. The abbreviation is missing a period. Write a period to fix it.

4. Piper likes Oct. because she likes the weather.
5. Toya wears boots in Feb. to keep her feet warm.
6. Yoshi has a party every Nov. for his birthday.

The Four Seasons

98 — Skill Sharpeners: Grammar and Punctuation • EMC 9951 • © Evan-Moor Corp.

Page 99

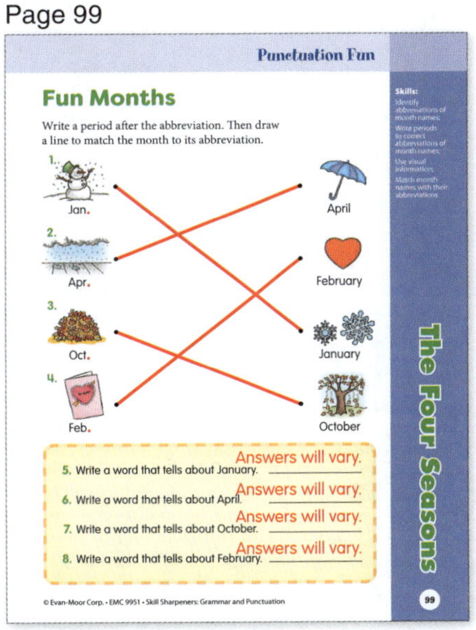
Punctuation Fun

Fun Months

Write a period after the abbreviation. Then draw a line to match the month to its abbreviation.

1. Jan. — January
2. Apr. — April
3. Oct. — October
4. Feb. — February

5. Write a word that tells about January. Answers will vary.
6. Write a word that tells about April. Answers will vary.
7. Write a word that tells about October. Answers will vary.
8. Write a word that tells about February. Answers will vary.

The Four Seasons

© Evan-Moor Corp. • EMC 9951 • Skill Sharpeners: Grammar and Punctuation — 99

Page 100

Review

Things We Like to Do

Use the verbs in the pencil to finish the sentences.

will build — jumped — steps

Write a verb that tells what is **happening now**.

1. Javier __steps__ by the fire on a cold day.

Write a verb that tells what **already happened**.

2. Sheila __jumped__ in a pile of leaves.

Write a verb that tells what **will happen**.

3. Sheila __will build__ a snowman.

Read the sentence. Does the month abbreviation have a period? Circle **yes** or **no**.

4. Apr 11 is my birthday. — yes / **no** (circled)
5. I went to school on Jan 2. — yes / **no** (circled)
6. On Oct. 3 I will go to a party. — **yes** (circled) / no

The Four Seasons

100 — Skill Sharpeners: Grammar and Punctuation • EMC 9951 • © Evan-Moor Corp.

Page 101

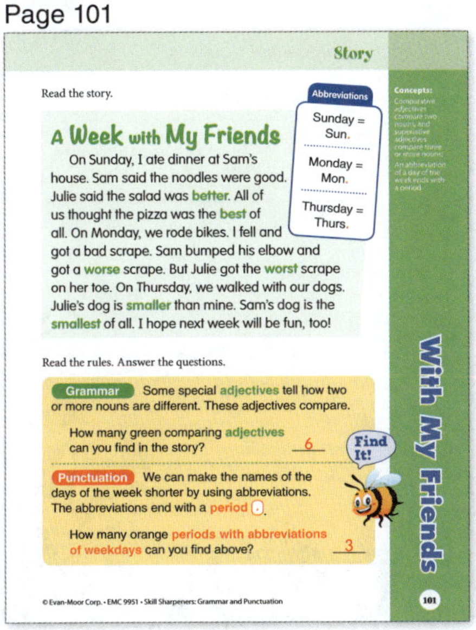
Story

Read the story.

A Week with My Friends

On Sunday, I ate dinner at Sam's house. Sam said the noodles were good. Julie said the salad was better. All of us thought the pizza was the best of all. On Monday, we rode bikes. I fell and got a bad scrape. Sam bumped his elbow and got a worse scrape. But Julie got the worst scrape on her toe. On Thursday, we walked with our dogs. Julie's dog is smaller than mine. Sam's dog is the smallest of all. I hope next week will be fun, too!

Abbreviations: Sunday = Sun. Monday = Mon. Thursday = Thurs.

Read the rules. Answer the questions.

Grammar: Some special adjectives tell how two or more nouns are different. These adjectives compare.

How many green comparing adjectives can you find in the story? __6__

Punctuation: We can make the names of the days of the week shorter by using abbreviations. The abbreviations end with a period.

How many orange periods with abbreviations of weekdays can you find above? __3__

Find It!

With My Friends

© Evan-Moor Corp. • EMC 9951 • Skill Sharpeners: Grammar and Punctuation — 101

Page 102

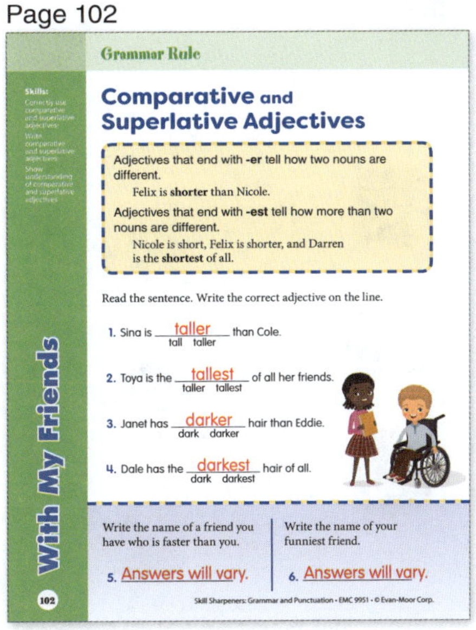
Grammar Rule

Comparative and Superlative Adjectives

Adjectives that end with **-er** tell how two nouns are different.
Felix is **shorter** than Nicole.

Adjectives that end with **-est** tell how more than two nouns are different.
Nicole is shorter, Felix is shorter, and Darren is the **shortest** of all.

Read the sentence. Write the correct adjective on the line.

1. Sina is __taller__ than Cole. (tall / taller)
2. Toya is the __tallest__ of all her friends. (taller / tallest)
3. Janet has __darker__ hair than Eddie. (dark / darker)
4. Dale has the __darkest__ hair of all. (dark / darkest)

Write the name of a friend you have who is faster than you.
5. Answers will vary.

Write the name of your funniest friend.
6. Answers will vary.

With My Friends

102 — Skill Sharpeners: Grammar and Punctuation • EMC 9951 • © Evan-Moor Corp.

Page 103

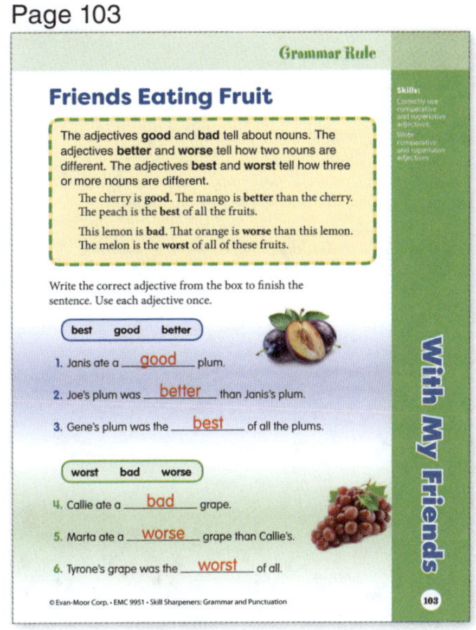
Grammar Rule

Friends Eating Fruit

The adjectives **good** and **bad** tell about nouns. The adjectives **better** and **worse** tell how two nouns are different. The adjectives **best** and **worst** tell how three or more nouns are different.

The cherry is **good**. The mango is **better** than the cherry. The peach is the **best** of all the fruits.

This lemon is **bad**. That orange is **worse** than this lemon. The melon is the **worst** of all of these fruits.

Write the correct adjective from the box to finish the sentence. Use each adjective once.

best — good — better

1. Janis ate a __good__ plum.
2. Joe's plum was __better__ than Janis's plum.
3. Gene's plum was the __best__ of all the plums.

worst — bad — worse

4. Callie ate a __bad__ grape.
5. Marta ate a __worse__ grape than Callie's.
6. Tyrone's grape was the __worst__ of all.

With My Friends

© Evan-Moor Corp. • EMC 9951 • Skill Sharpeners: Grammar and Punctuation — 103

To download a larger version of this answer key, go to: ***www.evan-moor.com/resources***
Enter your email address and this resource code: **EMC9951**

Page 104

Punctuation Rule

Periods with Abbreviations of Days of the Week

Each day of the week has an abbreviation. The abbreviation ends with a **period** (.).

Day of the Week	Abbreviation
Sunday	Sun.
Monday	Mon.
Tuesday	Tues.
Wednesday	Wed.
Thursday	Thurs.
Friday	Fri.
Saturday	Sat.

Write an abbreviation to answer the question.

1. What is the first day of the week? Sun.
2. What is the last day of the week? Sat.
3. What is the day before Thursday? Wed.
4. Which day of the week comes after Sunday? Mon.
5. Which day of the week comes before Friday? Thurs.

With My Friends

Page 105

Grammar Fun

All About My Friends

Read the questions. Then draw a picture of you and your friends. Last, answer the questions.

1. Who is the tallest? Answers will vary.
2. Who is the shortest? Answers will vary.
3. Who is the youngest? Answers will vary.
4. Who is the oldest? Answers will vary.
5. Who is shorter than you? Answers will vary.
6. Who is taller than you? Answers will vary.

Drawings will vary.

With My Friends

Page 106

Application

Write It Right!

The adjective in the sentence is wrong. It is underlined. Write the correct adjective on the line.

1. Kate is tallest than Paula. taller
2. Earl has the worse flu of all his friends. worst
3. Leah thinks Tony's house is gooder than Amy's house. better
4. Dom is the faster of all. fastest

Circle the day of the week in each sentence. Write the abbreviation on the line.

5. On (Tuesday) my friend is coming over. Tues.
6. Every (Friday) Joe eats dinner with us. Fri.
7. On (Saturday) I will sleep over at my friend's house. Sat.

With My Friends

Page 107

Punctuation Fun

One School Week

Read the notes on the classroom's board. Then answer the questions. Use the abbreviation for the day of the week, and use a period.

Monday, April 2 — School Play
Tuesday, April 3 — Eat Lunch with Mrs. Ray's Class
Wednesday, April 4 — P.E. Day
Thursday, April 5 — Music Day
Friday, April 6 — Shelly's Birthday

1. What day is the school play? Mon.
2. What day is Shelly's birthday? Fri.
3. What day is P.E. Day? Wed.
4. What day is Music Day? Thurs.

With My Friends

Page 108

Review

Funny Friends

Answer the items.

1. Write the name of someone you know who is funnier than a clown. Answers will vary.
2. Write one thing that is taller than your best friend. Answers will vary.
3. Write the fastest animal you know. Answers will vary.

Write 3 sentences. In each sentence write one thing you do on a day of the week. Use an abbreviation for the day of the week. Remember to use a period.

4. Answers will vary.
5. Answers will vary.
6. Answers will vary.

With My Friends

Page 109

Story

Read the text.

What About Bugs?

Do you think some bugs look scary? Yes, bugs can make some people feel afraid. But some bugs look pretty. There are many different kinds of bugs. Have you ever seen a beetle? Yes, the picture shows a beetle. It is a large bug. Do you think all beetles are the same? No, they are not. What bugs have you seen? You have probably seen an ant before. Ants and other bugs are important. Do you know why? Yes, they help keep the planet clean and green!

Read the rules. Answer the questions.

Find It!

Grammar: We use the words **a**, **an**, and **the** before nouns.

How many green words can you find in the text?
a 3 an 1 the 3

Punctuation: We use a **comma** after the words **yes** and **no** in a sentence.

How many **commas** can you find after **yes** and **no** in the text? 4

Bugs and Insects

Page 110

Grammar Rule

Articles

We use the words **a** and **an** before words that name one person, place, animal, or thing. Use **an** for words that begin with **a**, **e**, **i**, **o**, or **u**.

A worm has no legs. An ant has six legs.

We can use the word **the** before singular and plural naming words. Mostly we use **the** to tell about a special person or thing.

The bee buzzes. The insect flies. The ants work.

Finish the sentence. Write **a** or **an** before a word that names one. Write **the** before a word that names one or more than one.

1. A fruit worm eats an or the apple.
2. The grasshoppers will eat the plants.
3. A bee gets food from a or the flower.
4. A tick gets food from an or the animal.
5. A moth is an insect that gets food from plants.
6. Flies land on the bits of food they find.

Bugs and Insects

Page 111

Grammar Practice

Buggy Words

Write **a** or **an** before words that name one. Write **the** before words that name one or more than one.

1. the termites
2. a or the wasp
3. an ant
4. a or the fly
5. an or the earwig
6. the beetles

Bugs and Insects

Page 112

Punctuation Rule

Commas with Yes and No

Some sentences answer a question with **yes** or **no**. Use a **comma** after the words **yes** and **no** in a sentence.

Yes, that is a grasshopper.
No, that is not a termite.

Read the sentence. Then write a comma after **yes** or **no**.

1. No, a fly is not a beetle.
2. Yes, some beetles are black.
3. Yes, crickets can chirp.
4. No, honeybees do not live in a house.
5. Yes, wasps can sting.
6. Yes, caterpillars can crawl.
7. Yes, moths have wings.

Bugs and Insects

To download a larger version of this answer key, go to: ***www.evan-moor.com/resources***
Enter your email address and this resource code: **EMC9951**

Page 113

Grammar Fun

Make a Bug

Look at the word in the box. Draw to make the word look like a bug. Then write a sentence about the bug you drew. Use **a**, **an**, or **the** in your sentence.

Example: the — The fly goes up.

1. a — Answers will vary.
2. an — Answers will vary.
3. the — Answers will vary.

Bugs and Insects

© Evan-Moor Corp. • EMC 9951 • Skill Sharpeners: Grammar and Punctuation 113

Page 114

Application

Write It Right!

The sentence has a word that is wrong. It is underlined. Write the correct word on the line. Use a capital letter.

1. An grasshopper can jump. — A or The
2. A bees that make honey work hard. — The
3. A ant can carry food. — An or The

The sentence is missing a comma after **yes** or **no**. Write the comma in the sentence.

4. Yes, some bugs can bite.
5. No, worms do not have arms, legs, or eyes.
6. Yes, butterflies have colors on their wings.

Bugs and Insects

114 Skill Sharpeners: Grammar and Punctuation • EMC 9951 • © Evan-Moor Corp.

Page 115

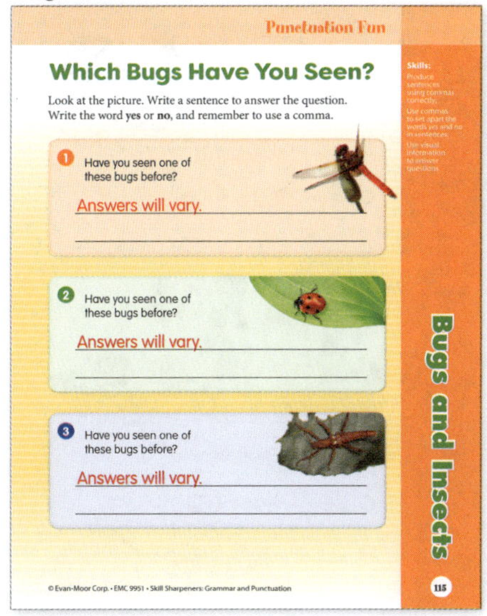
Punctuation Fun

Which Bugs Have You Seen?

Look at the picture. Write a sentence to answer the question. Write the word **yes** or **no**, and remember to use a comma.

1. Have you seen one of these bugs before? — Answers will vary.
2. Have you seen one of these bugs before? — Answers will vary.
3. Have you seen one of these bugs before? — Answers will vary.

Bugs and Insects

© Evan-Moor Corp. • EMC 9951 • Skill Sharpeners: Grammar and Punctuation 115

Page 116

Review

Bugs, Bugs, Everywhere!

Write a sentence. Use a word from the word box. Use **a**, **an**, or **the** in your sentence.

bees worm ant

1. Answers will vary.
2. Answers will vary.
3. Answers will vary.

Write a sentence to answer the question. Write the word **yes** or **no** in the sentence. Remember to use a comma.

4. Do you like bugs? — Answers will vary.
5. Would you pick up a caterpillar? — Answers will vary.

Bugs and Insects

116 Skill Sharpeners: Grammar and Punctuation • EMC 9951 • © Evan-Moor Corp.

Page 117

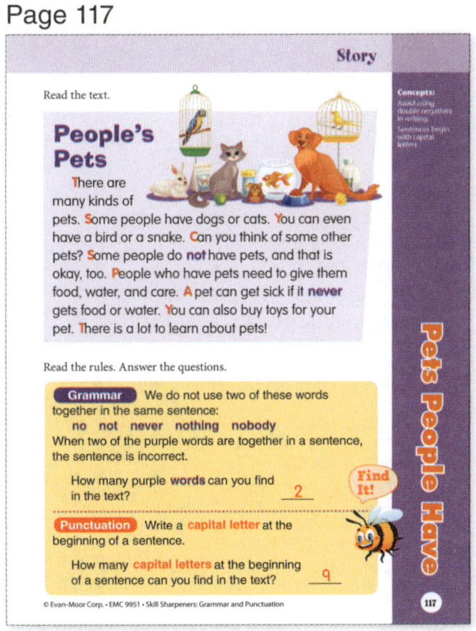
Story

Read the text.

People's Pets

There are many kinds of pets. Some people have dogs or cats. You can even have a bird or a snake. Can you think of some other pets? Some people do not have pets, and that is okay, too. People who have pets need to give them food, water, and care. A pet can get sick if it never gets food or water. You can also buy toys for your pet. There is a lot to learn about pets!

Read the rules. Answer the questions.

Grammar We do not use two of these words together in the same sentence: no not never nothing nobody
When two of the purple words are together in a sentence, the sentence is incorrect.
How many purple words can you find in the text? — 2

Punctuation Write a capital letter at the beginning of a sentence.
How many capital letters at the beginning of a sentence can you find in the text? — 9

Pets People Have

© Evan-Moor Corp. • EMC 9951 • Skill Sharpeners: Grammar and Punctuation 117

Page 118

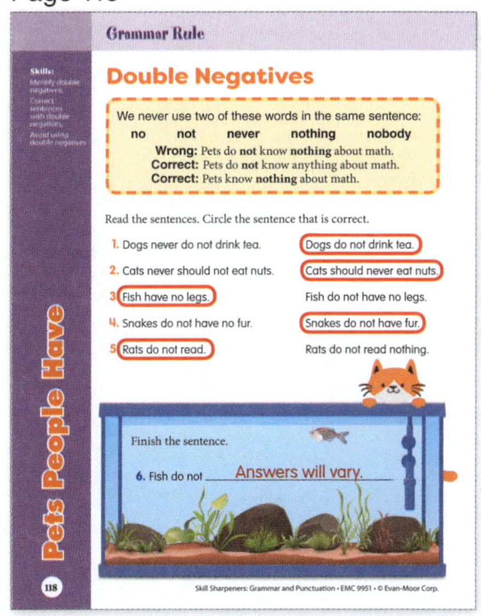
Grammar Rule

Double Negatives

We never use two of these words in the same sentence.
no not never nothing nobody
Wrong: Pets do **not** know **nothing** about math.
Correct: Pets do **not** know anything about math.
Correct: Pets know **nothing** about math.

Read the sentences. Circle the sentence that is correct.

1. Dogs never do not drink tea. / **Dogs do not drink tea.** (circled)
2. Cats never should not eat nuts. / **Cats should never eat nuts.** (circled)
3. **Fish have no legs.** (circled) / Fish do not have no legs.
4. Snakes do not have no fur. / **Snakes do not have fur.** (circled)
5. **Rats do not read.** (circled) / Rats do not read nothing.

Finish the sentence.

6. Fish do not Answers will vary.

Pets People Have

118 Skill Sharpeners: Grammar and Punctuation • EMC 9951 • © Evan-Moor Corp.

Page 119

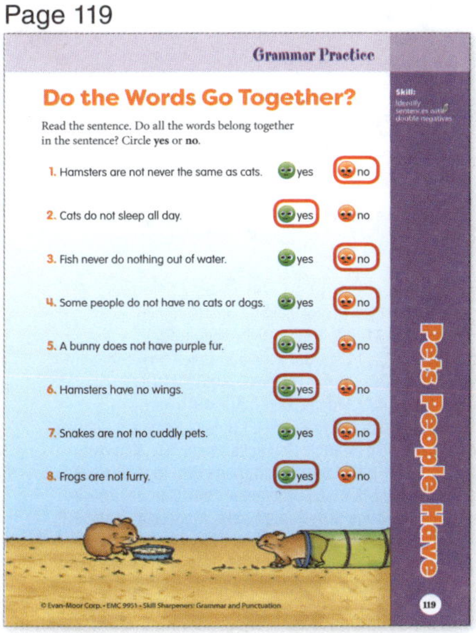
Grammar Practice

Do the Words Go Together?

Read the sentence. Do all the words belong together in the sentence? Circle **yes** or **no**.

1. Hamsters are not never the same as cats. — no
2. Cats do not sleep all day. — yes
3. Fish never do nothing out of water. — no
4. Some people do not have no cats or dogs. — no
5. A bunny does not have purple fur. — yes
6. Hamsters have no wings. — yes
7. Snakes are not no cuddly pets. — no
8. Frogs are not furry. — yes

Pets People Have

© Evan-Moor Corp. • EMC 9951 • Skill Sharpeners: Grammar and Punctuation 119

Page 120

Punctuation Rule

Mechanics: Capital Letters in Sentences

All sentences begin with a **capital letter**.
Telling sentence: A dog has a tail.
Asking sentence: Do bunnies have tails?

Write the correct word to finish the sentence.

1. Some pets like to play with people. (Some some)
2. Dogs can have dreams. (dogs Dogs)
3. Cats can see well in the dark. (Cats cats)
4. Bunnies take a lot of naps. (bunnies Bunnies)
5. Many fish can smell things. (Many many)

Pets People Have

120 Skill Sharpeners: Grammar and Punctuation • EMC 9951 • © Evan-Moor Corp.

Page 121

Grammar Fun

Note for the Dog Walker

Read the note. It tells how to take care of a dog. In each sentence, cross out the word that doesn't belong.

Instructions For Dog Walker
1. You should ~~not~~ never let the dog off its leash.
2. You can never ~~not~~ leave the dog alone for 8 hours.
3. The dog should ~~not~~ eat nothing at the table.
4. The dog should not have ~~no~~ juice.

Draw a picture of a person walking a dog.

Drawings will vary.

Pets People Have

© Evan-Moor Corp. • EMC 9951 • Skill Sharpeners: Grammar and Punctuation 121

To download a larger version of this answer key, go to: ***www.evan-moor.com/resources***
Enter your email address and this resource code: **EMC9951**

Page 122

Application

Skills:
Identify double negatives;
Identify capitalization errors

Write It Right!

Read the sentence. It has words that do not belong together. Circle the two words that should not be in the same sentence.

1. It's (not) safe for (nobody) to have a tiger as a pet.
2. Fish can (never) (not) play out of water.
3. Hamsters do (not) like to share (no) food with other hamsters.

Read the sentence. Circle the words that should not have a capital letter. Underline the words that need a capital letter.

4. some people have a (Pet) monkey.
5. pets can come in different (Sizes).
6. special animal doctors help us (Take) care of our pets.

Pets People Have

122 Skill Sharpeners: Grammar and Punctuation • EMC 9951 • © Evan-Moor Corp.

Page 123

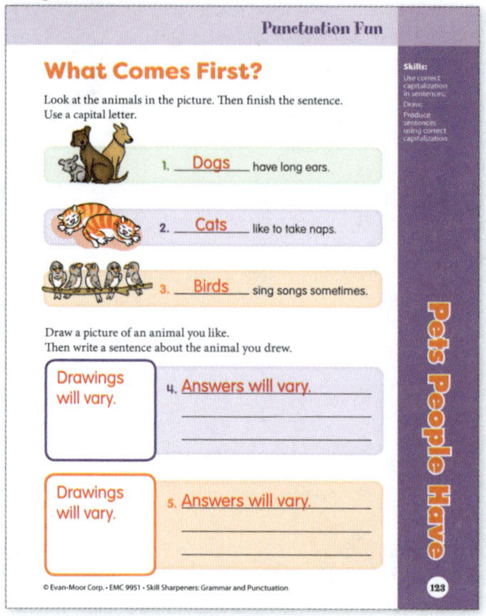
Punctuation Fun

What Comes First?

Look at the animals in the picture. Then finish the sentence. Use a capital letter.

1. Dogs have long ears.
2. Cats like to take naps.
3. Birds sing songs sometimes.

Draw a picture of an animal you like.
Then write a sentence about the animal you drew.

Drawings will vary.
4. Answers will vary.

Drawings will vary.
5. Answers will vary.

Skills:
Use correct capitalization in sentences;
Draw;
Produce sentences using correct capitalization

Pets People Have

© Evan-Moor Corp. • EMC 9951 • Skill Sharpeners: Grammar and Punctuation 123

Page 124

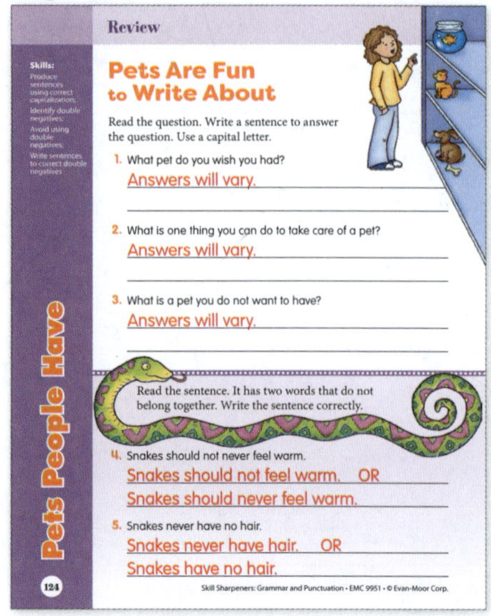
Review

Skills:
Produce sentences using correct capitalization;
Identify double negatives;
Avoid using double negatives;
Write sentences to correct double negatives

Pets Are Fun to Write About

Read the question. Write a sentence to answer the question. Use a capital letter.

1. What pet do you wish you had?
Answers will vary.
2. What is one thing you can do to take care of a pet?
Answers will vary.
3. What is a pet you do not want to have?
Answers will vary.

Read the sentence. It has two words that do not belong together. Write the sentence correctly.

4. Snakes should not never feel warm.
Snakes should not feel warm. OR
Snakes should never feel warm.
5. Snakes never have no hair.
Snakes never have hair. OR
Snakes have no hair.

Pets People Have

124 Skill Sharpeners: Grammar and Punctuation • EMC 9951 • © Evan-Moor Corp.